MW01089436

More than **200,000** student reviews on nearly **7,000** schools!

SEE IT ALL ON COLLEGEPROWLER.COM!

This book only offers a glimpse at our extensive coverage of one school out of thousands across the country. Visit *collegeprowler.com* to view our full library of content for FREE! Our site boasts thousands of photos and videos, interactive search tools, more reviews, and expanded content on nearly 7,000 schools.

CONNECT WITH SCHOOLS
Connect with the schools you are most interested in and discover new schools that match your interests.

FIND SCHOLARSHIPS
We give away $2,000 each month and offer personalized matches from a database of more than 3.2 million other scholarships!

SELECT A MAJOR
We have information on every major in the country to help you choose your degree and plan your career.

USE OUR TOOLS TO HELP YOU CHOOSE
Compare schools side-by-side, estimate your chances of admission, and get personalized school recommendations.

To get started, visit _collegeprowler.com/register_

Brown University

Providence, RI

Written by Justin Kim, Matthew Kittay

Edited by the College Prowler Team

ISBN # 978-1-4274-0357-5

©Copyright 2011 College Prowler

All Rights Reserved
Printed in the U.S.A.
www.collegeprowler.com

Last updated: 3/23/2011

College Prowler®
5001 Baum Blvd.
Suite 750
Pittsburgh, PA 15213

Phone: (800) 290-2682
Fax: (800) 772-4972
E-Mail: info@collegeprowler.com
Web: www.collegeprowler.com

How this all started...

When I was trying to find the perfect college, I used every resource that was available to me. I went online to visit school Web sites; I talked with my high school guidance counselor; I read book after book; I hired a private counselor. Sure, this was all very helpful, but nothing really told me what life was like at the schools I cared about. These sources weren't giving me enough information to be totally confident in my decision.

In all my research, there were only two ways to get the information I wanted.

The first was to physically visit the campuses and see if things were really how the brochures described them, but this was quite expensive and not always feasible. The second involved a missing ingredient: the students. Actually talking to a few students at those schools gave me a taste of the information that I needed so badly. The problem was that I wanted more but didn't have access to enough people.

In the end, I weighed my options and decided on a school that felt right and had a great academic reputation, but truth be told, the choice was still very much a crapshoot. I had done as much research as any other student, but was I 100 percent positive that I had picked the school of my dreams?

Absolutely not.

My dream in creating College Prowler was to build a resource that people can use with confidence. My own college search experience taught me the importance of gaining true insider insight; that's why the majority of this guide is composed of quotes from actual students. After all, shouldn't you hear about a school from the people who know it best?

I hope you enjoy reading this book as much as we've enjoyed putting it together. Tell me what you think when you get a chance. I'd love to hear your college selection stories.

Luke Skurman
CEO and Co-Founder
luke@collegeprowler.com

Welcome to College Prowler®

When we created College Prowler, we felt it was critical that our content was unbiased and unaffiliated with any college or university. We think it's important that our readers get honest information and a realistic impression of the student opinions on any campus—that's why if any aspect of a particular school is terrible, we (unlike a campus brochure) intend to publish it. While we do keep an eye out for the occasional extremist—the cheerleader or the cynic—we take pride in letting the students tell it like it is. We strive to create a book that's as representative as possible of each particular campus. Our books cover both the good and the bad, and whether the survey responses point to recurring trends or a variation in opinion, these sentiments are directly and proportionally expressed through our guides.

College Prowler guidebooks are in the hands of students throughout the entire process of their creation. Because you can't make student-written guides without the students, we have students at each campus who help write, randomly survey their peers, edit, layout, and perform accuracy checks on every book that we publish. From the very beginning, student writers gather the most up-to-date stats, facts, and inside information on their colleges. They fill each section with student quotes and summarize the findings in editorial reviews. In addition, each school receives a collection of letter grades (A through F) that reflect student opinion and help to represent contentment or satisfaction for each of our 20 specific categories. Just as in grade school, the higher the mark the more content or more satisfied the students are with the particular category.

Each book is the result of endless student contributions, hundreds of pages of research and writing, and countless hours of hard work. All of this has led to the creation of a student information network that stretches across the nation to every school that we cover. It's no easy accomplishment, but it's the reason that our guides are such a great resource.

When reading our books and looking at our grades, keep in mind that every college is different and that the students who make up each school are not uniform—as a result, it is important to assess schools on a case-by-case basis. Because it's impossible to summarize an entire school with a single number or description, each book provides a dialogue, not a decision, that's made up of 20 different topics and hundreds of student quotes. In the end, we hope that this guide will serve as a valuable tool in your college selection process. Enjoy!

The College Prowler Team

Table of Contents

By the Numbers

School Contact

Brown University
One Prospect Street
Providence, RI 02912

Control:
Private Non-Profit

Academic Calendar:
Semester

Religious Affiliation:
None

Founded:
1764

Web Site:
www.brown.edu

Main Phone:
(401) 863-1000

Student Body

Full-Time Undergraduates:
6,014

Part-Time Undergraduates:
218

Total Male Undergraduates:
3,096

**Total Female
Undergraduates:**
3,495

Admissions

Acceptance Rate:
11%

Total Applicants:
24,988

Total Acceptances:
2,790

Freshman Enrollment:
1,494

Yield (% of admitted students who enroll):
54%

Applicants Placed on Waiting List:
1,400

Applicants Accepting a Place on Waiting List:
450

Students Enrolled from Waiting List:
73

Transfer Applications Received:
1,004

Transfer Applications Accepted:
90

Transfer Students Enrolled:
55

Transfer Application Acceptance Rate:
9%

SAT I or ACT Required?
Either

SAT I Range (25th–75th Percentile):
1990–2300

SAT I Verbal Range (25th–75th Percentile):
650–760

SAT I Math Range (25th–75th Percentile):
670–770

SAT I Writing Range (25th–75th Percentile):
670–770

ACT Composite Range (25th–75th Percentile):
29–34

ACT English Range (25th–75th Percentile):
29–35

ACT Math Range (25th–75th Percentile):
28–34

ACT Writing Range (25th–75th Percentile):
28–32

Top 10% of High School Class:
92%

Application Fee:
$75

Common Application Accepted?
Yes

Admissions Phone:
(401) 863-2378

Admissions E-Mail:
admissions_undergrad@
brown.edu

Admissions Web Site:
www.brown.edu/
Administration/Admission/

Regular Decision Deadline:
January 1

Must-Reply-By Date:
May 1

Financial Information
Out-of-State Tuition:
$38,848

Room and Board:
$10,280

Books and Supplies:
$1,266

Average Amount of Federal Grant Aid:
$3,735

Percentage of Students Who Received Federal Grant Aid:
14%

Average Amount of Institution Grant Aid:
$24,450

Percentage of Students Who Received Institution Grant Aid:
39%

Average Amount of State Grant Aid:
$911

Percentage of Students Who Received State Grant Aid:
4%

Average Amount of Student Loans:
$6,760

Percentage of Students Who Received Student Loans:
35%

Total Need-Based Package:
$30,588

Percentage of Students Who Received Any Aid:
57%

Financial Aid Forms Deadline:
February 1

Financial Aid Phone:
(401) 863-9922

Financial Aid E-Mail:
FinAid_Administrator@
brown.edu

Financial Aid Web Site:
https://financialaid.brown.
edu/cmx_content.aspx?cpId=
80

Academics

The Lowdown On...
Academics

Degrees Awarded
Bachelor's degree
Master's degree

Most Popular Majors
Biology and Biological Sciences
Economics and Econometrics
History, General
International Relations and National Security Studies

Majors Offered
Architecture and Planning
Arts
Biological Sciences
Business
Computer and Sciences
Education
Engineering
Environmental Sciences
Health Care
Languages and Literature
Mathematics & Statistics
Philosophy and Religion
Physical Sciences

Psychology & Counseling
Social Sciences & Liberal Arts
Social Services

Undergraduate Schools/Divisions
Undergraduate College

Full-Time Instructional Faculty
733

Part-Time Instructional Faculty
128

Faculty with Terminal Degree
95%

Average Faculty Salary
$107,284

Student-Faculty Ratio
9:1

Class Sizes
Fewer than 20 students: 71%
20 to 49 students: 20%
50 or more students: 9%

Full-Time Retention Rate
97%

Graduation Rate
94%

Remedial Services?
No

Academic/Career Counseling?
Yes

Instructional Programs
Occupational: No
Academic: Yes
Continuing Professional: No
Recreational/Avocational: No
Adult Basic Remedial: No
Secondary (High School): No

Special Credit Opportunities
Advanced Placement (AP) Credits: No
Dual Credit: No
Life Experience Credits: No

Special Study Options
Study abroad
Teacher certification (below the postsecondary level)

Best Places to Study

Center for Information Technology (CIT)
Dorm and study rooms
Rockefeller Library (the Rock)
Sciences Library (the Sci-Li)
Various cafés and coffee shops

Did You Know?

 Brown does not have any general course requirements. While you must complete a total of 30 courses and specific courses within a concentration (Brown's word for major), there are absolutely no course requirements. You'll never have to take another math or English class if you don't want to. This system, known as the New Curriculum, started in 1969.

In line with this educational philosophy, most classes at Brown can be taken with a grade option of A/B/C/No Credit or Satisfactory/No Credit.

If one of Brown's hundreds of concentrations doesn't appeal to you, you can make up your own. An independent concentration is a course of study designed by the student with the guidance of University professors and deans that combines classes from different concentrations to show relations and connections between different studies.

Students Speak Out On...
Academics

Q A Good Number of Premeds
Many people who are in biology are, by extension, premed. Because of Brown's flexible curriculum, many biology majors double major-- usually in a humanities or arts. The academics are decently challenging, and most of the intro courses are curved.

Q It's About the Process, Not the Result
Brown's very free about the academics. It gives students the option to take any class pass/fail. There are no general education requirements (just requirements within your major, and even then, you usually have a list of possible options that fulfill a requirement, as opposed to a single specific class). This allows students to take what they are interested in taking. Although there are a few majors, like engineering and computer science, that have a lot of in-major requirements, majors like these are few and far between. Normally, Comparative Literature students are free to take Blues, Macroeconomics, and Religious and Secular Approaches to Globalization (in the Judaic Studies Department) in a single year if they chose. Also, I feel there is definitely some grade inflation, so A's are pretty easy to come by. It's definitely about the process of learning, not the end grade.

Q AB Human Biology
Human Biology is a unique concentration because it is essentially half biological science and half humanities. It offers flexibility and is very interdisciplinary.

Q **Prepare for Confusion and Soul-Searching**

You can do whatever you want with the curriculum, but I'm not sure core requirements would be such a bad thing. I feel like I've not always had the kind of advising you need to get through a system that allows you to literally do anything. Brown has definitely shaken up my beliefs in what I want and who I am -- I just hope I get something back for it by the end. Another WEIRD thing I never would have thought I'd find bothersome, but do: you can take almost any class as a freshman. So you're looking around going "There are seniors here! If I'm getting an A, what am I working towards here?"

Q I didn't get a chance to develop close relationships with my professors freshman year, because I took a lot of big intro classes. I did take one class where the professor led the sections and really got to know the students by taking pictures of all the students and putting our names on them, so when he called on someone, he knew who it was. It was a smaller class, but I felt like I got to know him that way.

Q I can go to lectures and classes at RISD. As a visual art major, that's a big plus. Access to RISD is very useful, but it's definitely not easy. Scheduling and getting into classes can be complicated. But if you are persistent, there are tons of resources. You have to make it a priority.

Q The professors here are the professors that change your life.

Q Because there is no core curriculum, you aren't typically forced into any bad courses. The skills and styles of teachers at Brown vary widely—as they probably do everywhere. But Brown does tell you to judge for yourself. The first several weeks of every semester is a 'shopping period' during which you can try out as many classes as you can pack into your day. Not everyone shops around, but most students shop at least a little. Shopping can be extremely useful for weeding out the incoherent mumblers and the digressive babblers, and for hunting down the best teachers.

The College Prowler Take On...
Academics

At Brown, persistence and personal responsibility play a big role in defining your undergraduate career. Students are rewarded for learning to work within Brown's small and intimate academic departments. In other words, it is always possible to work the system. Students always have a good chance of getting into high-level classes, even if they are outside their concentration. Many students come to Brown uncertain of their concentrations, and many switch their concentrations more than once in their undergraduate career. Brown's academic philosophy encourages exploration into new areas of study, which can spark new interests or projects. In general, Brown believes that every student knows what's best for him or herself.

Unlike other elite universities, Brown's primary focus is on undergraduate students. In accordance with this goal, all Brown professors are required to teach an undergraduate class, which gives students access to some of the top academics in their field. Most students are able to make strong connections with at least a few professors who provide them with support as they develop their own interests. There are, of course, shortcomings to Brown's system. The lack of many professional schools, like law or a business school, can make the post-Brown transition a bit jarring. In addition, for a large university, Brown can sometimes seem to have a limited number of courses available, with some departments lacking a large enough staff to support all the students. Often, you have to try for several semesters to get into a popular or limited-enrollment class. However, with persistence, anything is possible at Brown.

The College Prowler® Grade on

Academics: A

A high Academics grade generally indicates that professors are knowledgeable, accessible, and genuinely interested in their students' welfare. Other determining factors include class size, how well professors communicate, and whether or not classes are engaging.

Local Atmosphere

The Lowdown On...
Local Atmosphere

City, State
Providence, RI

Setting
Mid-sized city

Distances to Nearest Major Cities
Boston – MA – 1 hour
New York City – NY – 4 hours

Points of Interest
Federal Hill
India Point Park
Lupo's at the Strand
Newport Beaches
Outdoor Ice Rink at Kennedy Plaza
Purgatory Chasm
The RISD Museum
Roger Williams Park Zoo
Waterplace Park

Shopping Centers

Providence Place Mall
Thayer Street
Wayland Square
Wickenden Street

Major Sports Teams

Boston Red Sox: baseball
New England Patriots:
football

Movie Theaters

Avon Cinema

260 Thayer St.
Providence
(401) 421-3315

The Cable Car Cinema

204 South Main St.
Providence
(401) 272-3970

The Castle Cinema

1039 Chalkstone Ave.
Providence
(401) 751-3456

Providence Place Cinema

10 Providence Pl.
Providence
(401) 270-4659

Did You Know?

5 Fun Facts about Brown:
- Providence hosts Waterfire on weekend nights in late spring, summer, and early fall. Ninety-seven bonfires line the river at Waterplace Park. Local residents enjoy the fires, music, and food vendors as they walk along the river. Artist Barnaby Evans, a Brown graduate, created Waterfire for the city's newly renovated riverside area in 1994.
- A few times a semester RISD, hosts a student art sale on Benefit Street. There's no better place to buy your holiday or birthday presents.
- Brown is about a 10-minute walk from the world-famous Lupo's Heartbreak Hotel, where big and small shows, from punk to jazz, happen on an almost nightly basis.
- Once a month, Providence, hosts Gallery Night. Galleries around the city, including Brown's Bell Gallery, open their doors and wine cellars to locals who want to take in a little culture. Brown and RISD student art is almost always part of the event.
- Recently, Providence has been the stage for numerous movies and TV shows. The obvious examples are the film Outside Providence and the show Providence on that was on NBC. Perhaps the most accurate portrayal of Providence is in Family Guy, which was written by a RISD graduate.

Local Slang:
Bubbler – a water fountain
Coffee Milk – like chocolate milk, but with coffee syrup
College Hill – the hill in Providence where Brown and RISD are located
Dropped Egg – a poached egg East Side – the gentrified side of Providence where Brown is located
Extra, Extra – extra cream, extra sugar at Dunkin' Donuts
Light and Sweet – coffee with cream and sugar at Rhode Island staple Dunkin' Donuts
Projo – the Providence Journal
Quahog – a big clam
Roe Dylin – how the locals say where they're from
Stuffies – a stuffed quahog

Famous Rhode Islanders:
Harry Anderson, the Farrelly Brothers, Emeril Lagasse, H.P.
Lovecraft, and Samuel Slater

Students Speak Out On...
Local Atmosphere

◯ It's Your Call
Providence is a pretty good-sized city. And most things are close to campus. It's just a short bus ride or a 15-minute walk to the mall (with a multiplex), great restaurants, and pretty much whatever else you want. The train station is also close, and it's only an hour or so to Boston.

◯ It Is Such a Prestigious College That You Wouldn't Wanna Miss It.
Rhode Island is not much known for it's big city adventures but the university is located at the perfect place for students who want to study and the university itself offers so much more. It is the perfect environment.

◯ Love Prov.
As someone who was originally skeptical of this city I can definitely say there is much more than meets the eye. The diversity of Providence's residents and community issues make it a great place to enjoy, learn from, and affect. I highly recommend participating in the UCAAP pre-orientation program if you are interested in getting involved in community work as a freshman (you also get aligned with great advisors through this program). As far as musical entertainment goes Providence is okay. The venues are quality and the acts that come through are relatively diverse, however, Boston is not too far away and, as a bigger city, has a greater selection of things to do.

Q Attractions

There are great events like WaterFire and really nice places like Providence Place Mall, but Providence's attractions are limited. It would be nice if there were more attractions on College Hill other than what's on Thayer Street.

Q Providence is pretty much a college city. There isn't really much to do outside of the college campus. However, there are always plenty of activities happening on campus.

Q Brown is in its own, cute little area of Providence on Thayer Street, where there are plenty of restaurants and shops and a movie theater. Downtown is a great theater district and the largest mall in New England, but a lot of people tend to hang out on or around campus mostly. Sometimes people like to go to Boston on the weekends— it's only an hour away by community rail, and there's plenty to do there.

Q The mall is right here. You really need to get off campus sometimes, but you don't have to go that far; downtown is great.

Q I love Thayer Street. There's so much to it. I've never been anywhere quite like it.

The College Prowler Take On...
Local Atmosphere

Providence is a city, but it's not a big city. Sometimes the desire for the city to grow and incorporate new and exciting features is at odds with its efforts to maintain the small-town feel. If you want to go to a club one night, a museum the next day, a hip-hop show, and eat a few meals, you can cram it all into a weekend. Some Brown students never really explore the city, let alone the places less than an hour's drive in any direction from College Hill. There are beaches, state parks, ski areas, and vineyards close enough to make day trips to, all surrounded by quaint New England towns. Students complain about the lack of drive-in theaters or an all-night diner, without realizing that there are several of both about 10 minutes away. There are more hip-hop, 80s, and live rock clubs and bars within walking distance of the University than Brown students can handle. And, of course, there is New York City and Boston, both easily accessible by bus and train for weekends when you need to get away.

Providence is a crowd pleaser. People from small towns may be a little intimidated at first, but except on goth night at Club Hell, the locals don't bite. Students from megalopolises such as New York, DC, or LA may scoff at the downtown area, which can be traversed in about 20 minutes, but no Brown student who puts in a little effort can honestly complain that there's nothing to do in Providence. The city simply has too much history, too many quirks, and too much to offer for the intrepid Brown student to find it boring.

A-

The College Prowler® Grade on

Local Atmosphere: A-

A high Local Atmosphere grade indicates that the area surrounding campus is safe and scenic. Other factors include nearby attractions, proximity to other schools, and the town's attitude toward students.

Health & Safety

The Lowdown On...
Health & Safety

Security Office
Department of Public Safety
75 Charlesfield St.
(401) 863-3103
*www.brown.edu/
Administration/Public_Safety*

Safety Services
Bike registration
Blue-light phones
Emergency e-mail notification
Operation ID Program
Rape Aggression Defense
courses
Safe Walk escort program
safeRIDE shuttle

Crimes on Campus
Aggravated Assault: 0
Arson: 1
Burglary: 83
Murder/Manslaughter: 0
Robbery: 0
Sex Offenses: 4
Vehicle Theft: 7

Health Center
Health Services
Andrews House
(401) 863-3953
*www.brown.edu/Student_
Services/Health_Services*
Monday–Friday 9:30
a.m.–4:30 p.m., Saturday 10
a.m.–3:30 p.m.

Health Services
24-hour EMS response
24-hour on-site nurse
Allergy testing
Birth control counseling
Dermatology clinic
Health education programs
Health forms for travel,
employment, and school
applications
Immunizations
Lab services
Pharmacy
Routine sports and travel
physicals
STD screenings
Women's health
X-ray

Day Care Services?
No

Students Speak Out On...
Health & Safety

Q Police and Safety Services at Brown
I would have to say that Brown provides services to keep students safe but we are always encouraged to take personal safety measures (carry a whistle, walk in groups, etc.). We have SafeRide that travels all around campus to pick up students. We also have shuttle services students can call. In addition, there is SafeWalk (people walk students to necessary destinations) and emergency poles all around campus.

Q Safe
I feel pretty safe walking around Brown. The only people who get mugged are people walking around by themselves after midnight. Brown does not care if you smoke pot or drink.

Q Safe School-Too Many Thieves
I think my school security is good. When there is fights and/or riots they are broken up quickly. I feel safe enough at school but do not ever leave anything valuable around because it will get taken.

Q Moderately Safe
I rarely feel unsafe, but the frequency of theft and crime in and around campus can be alarming, especially late at night.

Q I think that there are certain areas off campus that you should avoid when you are walking alone, but on campus, you don't have to worry about much.

Q I feel safe here. Then again, I'm from New York City, so I feel safe just about anywhere.

Q I don't think there is a reason to feel unsafe, but at the same time, if you are walking alone on Benefit Street at four in the morning on a Saturday and something happens to you, you cannot blame it on the area. You know the east is safer than any other area of Providence. I'm convinced that the men in yellow coats aren't doing much of anything.

Q Last year it really felt like there were e-mails coming every day about students getting jacked.

The College Prowler Take On...
Health & Safety

Brown students receive an alert by e-mail every time there is a major crime committed on campus or the University perceives a specific safety threat. Recently, in response to a real and perceived increase in crime on and around campus, Brown increased the hours of campus police, hired security officers to patrol at night, and hired a private consulting firm to address the problems. The University tries very hard to inform the students about the status of crimes on campus and provides services to encourage smart and safe movement on campus at night. The shuttle runs on a route all the way around campus and comes about every five minutes until 3 a.m. The escort, who picks up and drops off students from off-campus housing to any location on campus, runs every night from 5 p.m. until 3 a.m. Safe Walk is a student-run volunteer program that provides walking escorts for students every night. Students should feel safe, but not be naïve about the threats that do exist in cities and on College Hill.

The campus area has all the common security features. There are many blue-light phones and well-lit public areas, and the police presence is generally strong enough to deter crime. Most students seem to feel very safe on campus and will admit that things like theft happen when doors are carelessly left unlocked or valuables are left in public places. Still, many students choose to leave their laptops unattended in the libraries or never lock their dorm rooms.

The College Prowler® Grade on
Health & Safety: C+

A high grade in Health & Safety means that students generally feel safe, campus police are visible, blue-light phones and escort services are readily available, and safety precautions are not overly necessary.

Computers

The Lowdown On...
Computers

Wireless Access
Yes: Available in all dorms, dining halls, libraries, most cafés, and major campus locations.

24-Hour Labs?
Yes: Center for Information Technology (CIT) Building

Charged to Print?
Yes: Single-sided pages are 5 cents, double-sided pages are 7 cents. Each student is issued a $25 card at the begining of the year.

Special Software & Hardware Discounts

Adobe Creative Suite, Adobe Pro, ColdFusion, Director, DV Rack, Encore, FrameMaker, InDesign, Macromedia FreeHand, Office Standard Suite, Office Mac, Ovation, PageMaker, Photoshop, Soundbooth, RoboHelp Server

Did You Know?

Brown has a pioneering computer science department. One interesting ongoing project on campus is the Cave, an eight-foot cubicle where high-resolution stereo graphics are projected onto three walls and the floor to create a virtual-reality experience. The Cave is used for medical, archeological, artistic, and creative writing projects.

Students Speak Out On...
Computers

Q Plenty of Computer Labs Available Throughout Campus

Computer labs are plentiful throughout the campus, with little to no problems accessing one if needed. Of course, the majority of students have their own computer so I'm sure this helps to minimize the availability problem

Q Labs

Most of the labs are found in the libraries. They do get crowded during crunch times like finals and midterms. However most people have laptops. It would be best to have one of your own to use when writing papers and whatnot. But if you don't have one, it's not a huge problem. The labs are nice, especially the one in the SciLi. You get $30 worth of printing credit for each year, and each page is only 10 cents so it's a pretty good deal. There are also copy machines and scanners. Scanner usage is free. There's a really nice Mac lab too.

Q Good Wireless Access

Sometimes the wireless is slow, but it's available everywhere on campus, even the greens, which is great. The computer labs are never full and printing is fairly simple. I have a printer in my room, but I hardly ever use it because the library printers are faster and print double-sided.

Q

I'm a Mac user, and I've found that there are fewer resources available to me.

Q Definitely bring your own computer. The computer clusters are accessible and generally easy to use, but in college, everything depends on e-mail—you need to be able to access it at any hour.

Q Computers in the SciLi are always crowded. Bring your own computer, but if you don't have one, it should be okay. WiFi is great pretty much everywhere.

Q The computer clusters are crowded at certain times of day, but you can find a free space somewhere most of the time. It's definitely worth having your own computer in your room though. And there's free wireless everywhere on campus.

Q The network is great. Brown does a fairly good job of making sure the community doesn't have access to our over-the-top WiFi speed, so for better or worse we benefit from it. Computers are always available in the SciLib, but bringing your own computer is really a must.

The College Prowler Take On...
Computers

Computers are a necessary tool at Brown. All papers, research, and communication revolve around having access to computers. The Center for Information Technology helps students adapt their own computers for use in the University network. Every Brown student has a University e-mail account, server space, and full access to most of the University's computer software and hardware. All of this is in addition to the electronic research tools available through JOSIAH, the library Web site server. The CIT also holds free group and individual training sessions to help students use specific software that the University makes available through their network. Network security is high, which has the positive effect of keeping viruses and junk mail away from people's inboxes, but also has essentially cut off illegal file sharing on the University's network.

While many students get by without a computer, the majority of students either bring a computer or purchase one from the Brown bookstore's computer center or a private company soon after they arrive. The fact that most students have their own computer decreases the traffic at the clusters at all but the busiest times of the year. If you are buying a new computer, a laptop is your best bet—it takes up less space in the cramped freshman rooms and gives you the freedom to bring your computer to any of your favorite study spots. Brown's wireless network also gives students the chance to access the Internet with their laptop in certain places on campus. In general, Brown's computers offer more resources than most students could ever desire, and the school continues to expand its computing facilities, taking advantage of new technology as it becomes available.

B+

The College Prowler® Grade on
Computers: B+

A high grade in Computers designates that computer labs are available, the computer network is easily accessible, and the campus's computing technology is up-to-date.

Facilities

The Lowdown On...
Facilities

Campus Size
140 acres

Student Centers
Faunce House

Main Libraries
Art Slide Library
John Hay Library (Special
Collections)
Orwig Music Library
Rockefeller Library (The Rock)
Sciences Library (SciLi)

**Service & Maintenance
Staff**
519

Popular Places to Chill
Common areas
Dorms
Social events

Bar on Campus

Faunce House
The Graduate Center Bar

Bowling on Campus

None

Coffeehouse on Campus

A small coffee and snack shop in the lobby of the Rockefeller Library
Coffeeshop in Brown Bookstore
The Upper Blue Room in Faunce House

Movie Theater on Campus

The Brown Film Society has movie marathons in the evenings and on the weekend in Carmichael Auditorium.

Favorite Things To Do

The diversity of interests in the student body and the vast number of options available to students means that you'll probably end up with a regular list of activities that you enjoy doing. The specifics will differ from person to person, but every student seems to keep busy somehow. Unless you make an effort to do so, don't worry about a lack of things to do. While at Brown, you will probably never find yourself idle with nothing to do. There are a great number of student organizations for a wide multitude of interests. You will most likely find at least a few that interest you, and if not, you can form your own.

Students Speak Out On...
Facilities

Q Brown University Libraries

Brown has a multitude of resources at each library to assist students. The two main libraries are the Rockefeller Library and the Sciences Library. There are great study rooms (group and individual) and amazing resources (books and internet) to help students research for papers or projects.

Q Sometimes Better Than Others

The buildings aesthetically are wonderful, though the insides are not always the best, but they're definitely workable. The athletic center is really nice, and the libraries are too. Campus activities are lively and fun.

Q The Campus as a Whole Is Beautiful

Brown has a gorgeous campus that has a nice mix of open green spaces and big shopping streets. The campus buildings are a variety of architectural styles but come together nicely. While the dorms are not very new, they tend to be spacious.

Q

The facilities are very nice. They're very state-of-the-art and Ivy League-ish. We don't have an official student center, but Faunce Hall acts as one, since it houses the Student Activities Office, the mail room, a mini-arcade, the Campus Market, and various other things.

Q

Brown needs a better central place, something like a student center or rec center.

Q

The facilities are amazing and high tech.

Q There is one main gym, as well as several smaller satellite gyms spread out across campus. The libraries are adequate places to study, although you don't really need to go all the way to a library to study—there are nice, quiet lounges in most dorms. We don't really have a student center, unfortunately, but there's not that much need for one considering all the convenient places to study, eat, and hang out.

Q The gym is old and not so nice. Some of the athletic fields are really far away. The satellite facilities are a little nicer, though, but they are small. The libraries are fantastic, and the student center has been redone recently. Basically, the athletic facilities are great. The sports, not so much.

The College Prowler Take On...
Facilities

Brown's facilities reflect Brown student's needs—the average Brown student would tell you they spend much more time in the library than at the gym. Therefore, it makes sense that the libraries and computer centers are constantly renovated and updated, while other facilities may receive less attention. That being said, Brown is not completely lacking any facilities, but it is easy to see which interests are given priority.

Compared to other Ivies, Brown's facilities are modest and reflect a certain degree of frugality. A quick look at the campus will not necessarily showcase the hidden, but first-rate, costume shop, wood and metal working studio, or the special libraries. Most students have everything they need, though it may take them a little time to find it.

B

The College Prowler® Grade on
Facilities: B

A high Facilities grade indicates that the campus is aesthetically pleasing and well-maintained; facilities are state-of-the-art, and libraries are exceptional. Other determining factors include the quality of both athletic and student centers and an abundance of things to do on campus.

Campus Dining

The Lowdown On...
Campus Dining

Meal Plan Available?
Yes

24-Hour Dining
None

Average Meal Plan Cost
$3920 per year

Average Meals/Week
20

Freshman Meal Plan Required?
Yes

Dining Halls & Campus Restaurants

The Blue Room
Location: Faunce House, the Main Green
Food: Sandwiches, soup
Hours: Monday–Friday 7 a.m.–6 p.m.

Campus Market
Location: Under the Blue Room
Food: Cereal, dairy, dry goods
Hours: Monday–Friday 8 a.m.–11 p.m., Saturday–Sunday 2 p.m.–11 p.m.

The Gate
Location: Alumni Hall, Pembroke campus
Food: Pizza, subs
Hours: Monday–Friday 11 a.m.–2 a.m., Saturday 6 p.m.–2 a.m., Sunday 4 p.m.–2 a.m.

The Ivy Room
Location: Wriston Quad, below the Ratty
Food: Omelets, pizza, salad, smoothies, wraps
Hours: Monday–Friday 11:30 a.m.–1:45 p.m., 8 p.m.–12 a.m.

Josiah's (Jo's)
Location: Middle of Vartan Gregorion Quad
Food: Grill, soups, sushi, wraps
Hours: Daily 24 hours (food is not available 2 a.m.–6 a.m.)

The Sharpe Refectory (The Ratty)
Location: Wriston Quad, main campus
Food: Grill, kosher meals, trattoria, vegetarian
Hours: Monday–Saturday 7:30 a.m.–7:30 p.m., Sunday 10:30 a.m.–7:30 p.m.

The Verney-Woolley Dining Hall (The V-Dub)
Location: Emery-Woolley Hall, Pembroke Campus
Food: Fruit station, sandwich station, vegetarian meals
Hours: Monday–Friday 7:30 a.m.–9:30 a.m., 11 a.m.–2 p.m., 4:30 p.m.–7:30 p.m.

Student Favorites

The Blue Room
The Gate
The Ivy Room
Josiah's

Off-Campus Places to Use Flex Money

None

Special Options

If you don't feel like eating the regular dining hall food, a good number of restaurants have very central locations on campus. In addition, a number of trucks and food carts come out around mealtimes. Overall, there are plenty of options and variety to keep things fresh.

Did You Know?

There is a Ratty Recipe Repository link off of Brown's Daily Jolt Web site which has student-submitted recipes for meals using ingredients in the University's cafeteria. Recipes include "Curry Chicken Salad," "Fruity Desert Crepes," and "Macaratty and Cheese."

Students Speak Out On...
Campus Dining

Q I Like It.
I am a big fan of the food on campus, however, my parents were not the best cooks. My favorite things are the fact that you can make your own panini if you're not diggin the meal of the night and the Blue Room, which has (pricey) food from a great local bakery and Indian restaurant.

Q Pretty Repetitive
I'm only a freshman and I already feel like I have the Ratty's rotation memorized. The food is pretty good quality, but and if you're creative with the choices there's always something to eat.

Q Okay...
The food at the dining hall isn't that bad, but it's very bland! It gives you the chance to be creative with your food though. Brown University caters to Vegetarians, but if you're not one, it can sometimes be hard to find something really good to eat.

Q Could Be Better
The food is not the best but it serves it purpose. The menus are repetitive so students need to get creative if they want to enjoy something different. Food around campus is good but also gets tiring since there are a limited number of businesses available. In addition the school should have some type of collaboration with the businesses surrounding so that students could use their flex-points and meals outside of brown because meals and points often go to waste.

Q V-Dub, Jo's, and The Gate are good. The Ratty is less good.

Q The food is pretty tasty, with the V-Dub being the preferred of the two main dining halls. The Gate and Jo's have pretty good food at decent times. My only gripe would be the V-Dub being closed on weekends, so you have to resort to the Ratty, which is consistent but generally worse.

Q The traditional dining halls are decent—they always offer enough options to keep everyone happy. The informal eateries are all great, especially since they're open until 2 a.m. The Gate has great pizza and panini, Jo's has great burgers, quesadillas, and fresh salads, and the Ivy Room has great falafel. We also have a campus café called The Blue Room that has great coffee and pastries, and a campus pub called the Hourglass, which always has really great music on Saturday evenings.

Q The meal plans are complicated and convoluted but allow you to have a wide array of choices of where to eat a given meal. Besides the Ratty, which is basically a stereotypical college cafeteria, there is a smaller, cozier dining hall with better food, a pizza place, a vegetarian dining room, and many snack bars. The dining halls allow you to take a box of food with you instead of eating there, which is convenient. Being vegetarian is incredibly easy here because there are so many of us, and the dining services take that into account when devising meal plans.

The College Prowler Take On...
Campus Dining

While most schools have contracted with Marriott or fast-food companies for their dining needs, Brown prides itself on maintaining a University-run food service. Why exactly this is a source of pride is another question entirely. The main dining halls—the Ratty and the V-Dub—serve what can only be described as average food. Chances are, you won't return home for the holidays demanding your mom cook more like Brown Food Services (BFS). A lack of variety and the inability to use credits in real restaurants close to campus can be frustrating. The few cafés and restaurants run by the University are equally frustrating because they are more expensive than independent cafés and diners on Thayer and Wickenden Street. The Brown meal plan feels more like a middle school lunch program than a welcomed dining experience.

Year after year, the Ratty is the butt of new and old jokes, but as demonstrated by the Ratty Recipe Repository, many Brown students embrace the standard cafeteria-style eating. Besides, the meal plan provides much more than hot food every day. The meal plan is a state of mind. From your first week on meal plan, you will undoubtedly enjoy meals with friends, meet lots of new people, and sing karaoke with your fellow Brunonians at the V-Dub. Good or bad, surviving meal plan freshman year is a defining experience and undoubtedly a right of passage. In time, however, you'll find the right balance of splurging for off-campus meals and eating creatively at the dining halls. Students who are off the meal plan might enjoy better food, but it is costly and time-consuming to fend for yourself.

The College Prowler® Grade on
Campus Dining: B-

The grade on Campus Dining addresses the quality of both school-owned dining halls and independent on-campus restaurants as well as the price, availability, and variety of food.

Off-Campus Dining

The Lowdown On...
Off-Campus Dining

Restaurant Listings

Al Forno
Food: Contemporary Italian
577 S. Main St., Downtown
(401) 273-9760
Price: $15–$50
Cool Features: Nothing
says your parents love you
like a dinner excursion to
Al Forno. Their brick-oven
pizza is world-famous and the
chocolate soufflé is a must.

Antonio's Pizza
Food: Pizza
258 Thayer St., Providence
(401) 455-3600
Price: $3–$15

Apsara
Food: Cambodian,
Vietnamese, Thai, and
Chinese
716 Public St., Providence
(401) 785-1490
Price: $2–$10
Cool Features: Although
Apsara is a 10-minute drive
from campus, it is so good

that Brown students cram
into the restaurant every
night.

Bagel Gourmet Ole
Food: Bagels, Mexican
228 Thayer St., Providence
(401) 331-1311
Price: $5–$5
Cool Features: Interesting
mix: bagles and Mexican?
Who thought it would work,
but it does!

Bickford's Grille
Food: American
1460 Mineral Spring Ave.,
North Providence
(401) 353-9442
Price: $5–$15
Cool Features: Known for
great New England-style
breakfast—which is to say
breakfast with seafood
integrated into it. Bickford's is
also a great spot to hit after
the bars on weekends; they
also offer takeout, which is a
big plus.

Byblos
Food: Middle Eastern
235 Meeting St.
(401) 453-9727
www.providencebyblos.com
Price: $5–$10
Cool Features: This is also a
hookah bar.

Café Paragon and Viva
Food: American/
Mediterranean
234 Thayer St., College Hill
(401) 331-6200
www.paragonandviva.com
Price: $5–$15
Cool Features: Despite its
reputation as a favorite
haunt for Brown's children
of privilege, the food is very
affordable. After 10 p.m.,
Viva becomes a hip Euro club
scene.

Café Zog
Food: Café and coffee shop
239 Wickenden St.,
Providence
(401) 421-2213
Price: $2–$7
Cool Features: Zog features a
private back patio and table
service.

The Creperie
Food: Crepes and smoothies
82 Fones Alley (off Thayer),
College Hill
(401) 751-5536
Price: $2–$7
Cool Features: Located
right off Thayer Street, the
Creperie is a great option
for any meal of the day. Late
hours make it one of the
few places to get a post-bar
snack.

Cuban Revolution Café

Food: Cuban
149 Washington St.,
Providence
(401) 331-8829
Price: $2–$10
Cool Features: The brilliant cabana atmosphere with live music in the evenings makes eating a pressed Cuban sandwich, fried plantain chips, and flan a welcome treat. Wear camouflage on Saturdays or a Che Guevara print on Mondays for special discounts.

East Side Pockets

Food: Middle Eastern
278 Thayer St., Providence
(401) 453-1100
Price: $2–$5
Cool Features: East Side Pockets provides excellent service, great food, and personality that satisfies the demand for affordable munchies.

Fellini Pizzeria

Food: Pizza
166 Wickenden St.,
Providence
(401) 751-6737
Price: $2–$6
Cool Features: Fellini is ridiculously popular among students, and most agree it's some of the best pizza in New England (though it definitely has its detractors).

It's particularly popular around midnight and thereafter on Fridays.

The Garden Grille Café and Juice Bar

Food: Vegetarian and vegan cuisine
727 East Ave., Pawtucket
(401) 726-2826
Price: $2–$12
Cool Features: The menu makes it easy for people with all kinds of dietary concerns to eat hearty and tasty meals like Vegan Nachos Supreme, a veggie Rueben or a slice of dark chocolate cake.

Haven Brothers

Food: Diner
72 Spruce St. (sort of)
Fulton and Dorrance Sts.,
Providence
(401) 861-7777
Price: $2–$8
Cool Features: For starters, Haven Brothers is not as much a restaurant as a trolley with a diner in it. The establishment is over a hundred years old, and serves a very mixed crowd when it pulls up in front of City Hall and serves diner fare through the morning hours.

Hemenway's Seafood Grill and Oyster Bar

Food: Seafood

121 S. Main St., Providence
(401) 351-8570
Price: $15-$40
Cool Features: The raw bar at
Hemenway's offers more than
15 varieties of raw shellfish,
and the waterfront location
makes it a great spot for hip
students and Providence
yuppies alike.

India

Food: Indian and Pakistani
123 Dorrance St., Downtown
(401) 278-2000
Price: $10–$25
Cool Features: Providence,
particularly the area around
Brown, offers a few good
Indian restaurants. Although
India may be a few dollars
more than other options, the
food and the service make
India the nicest choice.

Julian's

Food: Gourmet/fusion bistro
food
318 Broadway Ave., Federal
Hill
(401) 861-1770
Price: $5–$15
Cool Features: Julian's
is true boho Providence
dining—greasy with a
silver spoon. Breakfast is
particularly good; you can
get eggs benedict with lox
and Bourson cheese hash
served in a hip, artsy Café.

Kabob and Curry

Food: Indian
261 Thayer St., Providence
(401) 273-8844
www.kabobandcurry.com
Price: $10–$20

Louis

Food: Diner
286 Brook St.
(401) 861-5225
Price: $5–$10

Mediterraneo

Food: Authentic Italian
134 Atwells Ave., Federal Hill
(401) 331-7760
Price: $15–$40
Cool Features: Mediterraneo
is one of the few restaurants
that features Italian-speaking
servers and authentic Tuscan
cooking. Many of the eateries
on Federal Hill claim to be
worth their extravagant price,
but Mediterraneo, with its
enormous portions, truly is.

Nice Slice

Food: Pizza
267 Thayer St., Providence
(401) 453-6423
www.niceslice.com
Price: $13–$20

Ri~Ra

Food: Irish Pub
50 Exchange Terrace,
Downtown
(401) 272-1953
Price: $5–$15

Cool Features: Ri~Ra is a lively pub, which is a favorite of college students and the Providence happy-hour set. Once you live in Providence, you'll know how unusual that is.

Sawaddee Thai Restaurant

Food: Thai
93 Hope St., Providence
(401) 831-1122
www.sawaddeerestaurant. com
Price: $2–$12
Cool Features: Brown students are lucky to have this authentic, family-run place so close to campus. The takeout is a godsend, and diners will be pleased to see the signature dishes served as spicy as they dare to request them.

Shanghai

Food: Chinese
272 Thayer St., Providence
(401) 331-0077
www.shanghairi.com
Price: $10–$15

Best Asian
Apsara

Best Breakfast
Julian's

Best Healthy
The Garden Grille Café

Best Pizza
Antonio's Pizza
Nice Slice

Best Wings
Ri~Ra

Best Place to Take Your Parents
Hemenway's Seafood Grill and Oyster Bar
Mediterraneo

24-Hour Dining
None near Brown

Other Places to Check Out
Au Bon Pain
Ben and Jerry's
Broad Street Tokyo
D'Angelo's
Gordito Burrito
Johnny Rockets
Meeting Street Café
Mia Sushi
Miss Fanny's Soul Food

Kitchen
Sakura
Smoothie King
Ten Prime Steak & Sushi

Grocery Stores
Eastside Marketplace
165 Pitman St.
(401) 831-7771

Super Stop & Shop
333 W. River St.
(401) 861-9300

Whole Foods Market
261 Waterman St.
(401) 272-1690

Students Speak Out On...
Off-Campus Dining

Q Thayer Street

Many locaitions very near campus. Some student discounts, some variety, anything on Thayer street is frequently traversed by Brown students.

Q Slightly Above Average

Most places on Thayer St (middle of campus) are slightly costly and provide average food, but are very convenient and significantly better than the dining halls. I like Haruki's Express, Iron Wok, and Phonatic.

Q There are plenty of good restaurants right here on Thayer Street. Kabob and Curry has amazing Indian food, and Byblos has great Middle Eastern food—and I'm from New York, so I'm picky about ethnic cuisine! Andreas and Paragon are also good. Downtown, there's a great restaurant called Local 121 that only uses locally grown foods, and it's absolutely delicious.

Q The restaurants around Thayer are some of the best in the city. There are not too many chains and not a lot of American food, but you'll likely be hitting staples like Louis, Kabob and Curry, and Shanghai quite a bit.

Q Thayer Street is one of my favorite place to eat in Providence. It has so many places to eat.

Q There's Indian, Mexican, Vietnamese, Chinese, cheap, expensive, you name it. I like Bagel Gourmet Ole the best because it's cheap delicious Mexican and bagels for breakfast, lunch, and dinner.

Q Providence can be kind of expensive, and the food can be a little monotonous.

Q On my Brown application, I literally said that one reason I wanted to come here was for the great Italian food in the area.

The College Prowler Take On...
Off-Campus Dining

Providence truly caters to the epicurean diner. One need not stray further than the College Hill and the Downtown areas to find all varieties of ethnic food, dining styles, and atmospheres. Without a doubt, Providence is host to an impressive number of off-campus restaurants that offer variety in terms of price and menus. Vegetarian, kosher, and all other diets can be easily accommodated. Great food is truly one of Providence's greatest assets.

The scariest thing about off-campus eating, however, is the lack of supermarkets that are easily within walking distance to campus. The closest supermarket is over a mile away, which will sound a lot worse in February when it snows and gets dark before dinner. There are a few specialty markets nearby, including a Saturday farmer's market at Hope High School, but you really need a car if you plan to cook on a regular basis.

The College Prowler® Grade on

Off-Campus
Dining: A-

A high Off-Campus Dining grade implies that off-campus restaurants are affordable, accessible, and worth visiting. Other factors include the variety of cuisine and the availability of alternative options (vegetarian, vegan, kosher).

Campus Housing

The Lowdown On...
Campus Housing

On-Campus Housing Available?
Yes

Campus Housing Capacity
4,643

Average Housing Costs
$6,360

Number of Dormitories
31

Number of Campus-Owned Apartments
2

Dormitories

Andrews Hall

Floors: 3
Number of Occupants: 166
Bathrooms: Shared by floor
Coed: Yes
Residents: Freshmen, upperclassmen
Room Types: Singles (upperclassmen), doubles (freshmen)
Special Features: Each room has a sink with a medicine chest, which is very rare for freshman rooms.

Barbour Hall

Floors: 1
Number of Occupants: 37
Bathrooms: Shared with adjoined room
Coed: Yes
Residents: Sophomores
Room Types: Singles, doubles
Special Features: Every room shares a sink, toilet, and shower with one other room. Rooms also feature an enormous walk-in closet.

Caswell Hall

Floors: 4
Number of Occupants: 90
Bathrooms: Shared by floor
Coed: Yes
Residents: Sophomores
Room Types: Doubles
Special Features: Caswell is split into three towers, and each room has a non-working but atmospheric fireplace.

Emery-Woolley Hall

Floors: 4
Number of Occupants: 227
Bathrooms: Shared by a cluster of about six students
Coed: Yes
Residents: Freshmen, upperclassmen
Room Types: Singles, doubles
Special Features: In the coldest depths of winter, living in the same building as the V-Dub Cafeteria will make you the envy of Pembroke Campus. There is also a huge common room with a working fireplace and an elevator.

Graduate Center Suites

Floors: 4 to 5
Number of Occupants: 120
Bathrooms: Shared by suite
Coed: Yes
Residents: Mostly sophomores
Room Types: Suites with singles
Special Features: It might look a little like a prison, but it provides a good way for sophomores to get singles.

Hegemen

Floors: 4
Number of Occupants: 70

Bathrooms: Shared by suite
Coed: Yes
Residents: Upperclassmen
Room Types: Suites with
mostly singles, some
independent singles and
doubles
Special Features: The
five Hegemen towers are
connected by underground
tunnels.

Hope College
Floors: 4
Number of Occupants: 76
Bathrooms: Shared by floor
Coed: Yes
Residents: Freshmen,
upperclassmen
Room Types: Singles,
doubles
Special Features: Hope
College is conveniently
located on the Main Green,
and residents can look
forward to a year of leisurely
strolling from their bedroom
to classes.

Keeney Quad (Archibald, Bronson, Everett, Jameson, Mead, and Poland)
Floors: 4
Number of Occupants: 597
Bathrooms: Shared by floor
Coed: Yes
Residents: Freshmen,
upperclassmen
Room Types: Singles,
doubles, triples
Special Features: About half
of the freshmen class lives
in the Keeney megaplex. To
support so many, the dorm
has a lot of common rooms,
storage rooms, kitchens, and
two private quads.

Littlefield Hall
Floors: 4
Number of Occupants: 50
Bathrooms: Shared by floor
Coed: Yes
Residents: Freshmen
Room Types: Doubles
Special Features: Littlefield
is open for winter break to
house student athletes. If
you're not a jock, you might
have one staying in your
room over the holidays.

Metcalf Hall
Floors: 4
Number of Occupants: 60
Bathrooms: Varies by floor
Coed: Yes
Residents: Upperclassmen
Room Types: Singles
Special Features: Metcalf is a
quiet dorm ideal for serious
students or light sleepers.
The top floor is reserved for
female students only.

Miller Hall
Floors: 4
Number of Occupants: 55
Bathrooms: Shared by floor
Coed: Yes
Residents: Graduate students
Room Types: Singles

Special Features: Miller includes laundry facilities and services, kitchens, an Ethernet connection in each room.

Minden Hall

Floors: 6
Number of Occupants: 80
Bathrooms: Shared by suite
Coed: Yes
Residents: Upperclassmen
Room Types: Singles, suites
Special Features: Minden was renovated in 2002. The top floors have great views of the city, but not all suites have equal accommodations. When choosing Minden in the lottery, scope out the rooms first.

Morris-Champlin

Floors: 4
Number of Occupants: 200
Bathrooms: Shared by cluster
Coed: Yes
Residents: Freshmen, upperclassmen
Room Types: Singles, doubles, suites
Special Features: This is one of the few dorms that has an elevator, which makes moving in a breeze. Since the first floor of Champlin used to be the Pembroke infirmary, some rooms on the first floor have their own bathroom.

New Pembroke 1, 2, 3, 4

Floors: 4
Number of Occupants: 193
Bathrooms: Shared by floor
Coed: Yes
Residents: Freshmen, Upperclassmen
Room Types: Singles, doubles
Special Features: New Pembroke may be at the edge of Pembroke campus, but it is on Thayer Street and close to restaurants and stores.

Perkins Hall

Floors: 4
Number of Occupants: 275
Bathrooms: Shared by floor
Coed: Yes
Residents: Freshmen
Room Types: Singles, doubles
Special Features: Perkins is strictly first-year housing shared only with upperclassman counselors. It is one of the furthest dorms from campus, but it is known for breeding camaraderie.

Slater Hall

Floors: 4
Number of Occupants: 50
Bathrooms: Shared by floor
Coed: Yes
Residents: Juniors, seniors
Room Types: Singles, doubles, triples
Special Features: This is

a favorite of juniors and seniors because it is right on the Main Green. Rooms are spacious with high ceilings and great views.

Vartan Gregorian Quad
Floors: 4
Number of Occupants: 290
Bathrooms: Shared by floor
Coed: Yes
Residents: Upperclassmen
Room Types: Three-, four-, five-, and six-person suites
Special Features: This housing complex forms a quad, and Josiah's is conveniently located in the center. Residents enjoy the use of elevators and large common rooms in their suites. The quad also houses the Brown Hotel where your parents can stay at a bargain price.

Wriston Quad (Buxton, Chapin, Diman, Goddard, Harkness, Marcy, Olney, Sears, Wayland)
Floors: 4 to 5
Number of Occupants: 743
Bathrooms: Shared by floor or suite
Coed: Yes
Residents: Freshmen, upperclassmen
Room Types: Singles, doubles, suites
Special Features: Wriston Quad has the advantage of

being near campus and the main dining hall. The singles and doubles are nothing special, but the suites on the top floors are arguably the nicest at Brown. Fraternities or sororities usually occupy the lower floors of the buildings, but they do not dominate the scene except during weekend parties.

Campus-Owned Apartments

Barbour Hall Apartments
Floors: 2
Number of Units: 129
Bathrooms: Private
Coed: Yes
Residents: Sophomores
Room Types: Apartments
Special Features: Each apartment has a kitchen, common room, and a private bathrooms.

Young Orchard Apartments
Floors: 4
Number of Units: 190
Bathrooms: Shared by apartment
Coed: Yes
Residents: Upperclassmen
Room Types: Apartments
Special Features: Basically the same as living in an off-campus apartment, but

it is close enough to campus
that students don't have to
worry about transportation.

Freshmen Required to Live on Campus?

Yes

Undergrads Living On Campus

80%

Best Dorms

Andrews Hall
Barbour Hall
Young Orchard Apartments

Worst Dorms

New Pembroke
Perkins Hall

What You Get

Bed
Bookshelf
Desk
Dresser
Ethernet connection
Lamp
Phone jack

Available for Rent

Microwaves, refrigerators

Did You Know?

Campus housing is the source of many of Brown's most popular rumors. There is a highly mysterious tunnel system that connects a good deal of Wriston Quad to the Greek and Program houses. There are endless theories about the original intent of these tunnels, but rumor has it they used to extend over a large portion of the school.

Brown is also said to have a few secret societies in addition to the well-publicized organizations; these societies are said to be located near campus in mysterious mansions. The most famous myth concerns the ominous Graduate Center Suites. It is rumored to have been designed in 1968 by prison architects as a fortress in case of riots. Regardless of the building's design intent, it is a fact that the imposing concrete spiral staircase was actually built incorrectly because the builders read the blueprints wrong.

After talking so much about housing, Brown students have come up with their own terms for Brown's sometimes odd dorms. A "dingle" is a room originally built as a double which has been converted to a single. A "trouble" is a room originally built as a double which has been converted to a triple.

Adding to the eccentricity of the Brown housing system, Residential Life sponsors a movie contest each year in February. The prize, which can go to any group, including rising sophomores, is the ability to select any on-campus room, suite, or apartment. As you would expect, this is a competitive contest.

Students Speak Out On...
Campus Housing

Q Life at Brown
Life at Brown Dorms is great. As many college dorms, there are big rooms, average rooms, and small rooms. The housing lottery for sophomores is a bit stressful, but everyone is guaranteed housing, and living on campus provides a great social atmosphere!

Q Campus Housing Is Very Good
all the dorms are very spacious. and everyone on campus is amazing

Q Dorms Are Better Than Expected
Brown dorms are a lot bigger than other schools i previously visited. Everyone definitely has a shot at a good dorm building not just upperclassmen. Housing Lottery is hectic and chaotic so a new system should be put in place so that students are less stressed out about the process. Locations are even except fr Perkins and Young Orchard which are both far from everything on campus.

Q Not Shabby
Freshman housing is great--rooms are big, everyone gets a double, and is living around other freshman. That said, dorms are not palaces, but they aren't the reason you come here

Q The dorms at Brown are very huge and very pretty.

Q Dorms are pretty decent. Some are much nicer than others, though. As a freshman, you'd want to be in Keeney—that's where most freshmen are, and it's located on the convenient side of campus.

Q All freshmen dorms are fine. Don't worry if you get a so-called 'bad dorm' because you end up bonding with your dormmates over that anyway. There is a housing shortage, but it's really the sophomores that get screwed. As a freshman, you have no control over what dorm you get, so don't worry about it.

Q Emery Woolley and Mo-Champ used to be super-gross, a bad '70s public-housing project. They refurnished them well. I'll cheer Keeney for its social, thirsty, and frisky freshmen. Since you don't pick housing as a freshman, have faith in Residential Life. Andrews has really nice rooms, but it's pretty quiet.

The College Prowler Take On...
Campus Housing

Brown guarantees housing for four years if a student wants it. The University also require that students live on campus the first six semesters of their Brown career. Although many students complain about this policy, it makes life easier for rising sophomores and juniors, and relieves a lot of the stress between freshman and junior year. Starting in the spring of freshman year, students are faced with a lot of choices in terms of housing. In addition to the lottery, all the program and Greek houses give students the choice of getting around the fickle lottery system. In addition to circumventing the lottery, special housing is one more chance to meet new people and have new experiences.

Despite complaints about the frustrating lottery system, Brown's housing system is better than most. After freshman year, the system can be worked to a student's advantage— including some houses reserved specifically for sophomores. Live in the dorms first year, then live in a house sophomore year. Move to a different program house junior year if you didn't love your sophomore digs. By senior year, you'll skip the whole lottery system and will be guaranteed prime on-campus housing without ever being forced to enter the lottery or move off campus. A little finesse is all it takes to make the housing system work for you.

The College Prowler® Grade on

Campus
Housing: A-

A high Campus Housing grade indicates that dorms are clean, well-maintained, and spacious. Other determining factors include variety of dorms, proximity to classes, and social atmosphere.

Off-Campus Housing

The Lowdown On...
Off-Campus Housing

Undergrads Living Off Campus
20%

Average Rents
Studio: $600
1 BR: $800
2 BR: $1,200

Best Time to Look for a Place
For the best selection, look no later than February; however, if you want the best prices, wait until late in the spring when the landlords are anxious to rent their spaces.

Popular Areas
Brook and Cushing Streets, right off Thayer
Fox Point, around Governor Street
Wickenden Street area

Students Speak Out On...
Off-Campus Housing

Q Off-Campus Housing
You should read the Brown Daily Herald for more information on housing. It's generally available, and here is off-campus housing on all sides of campus. There is a big range in quality and price-- you just don't want to be paying more for lower quality (which sometimes seems to be the case).

Q Nova Off-Campus Housing
It's sort of expensive, but it's close to the campus, there is laundry, it's safe, and neat.

Q Lots of Options Near Campus
There are lost of apartments available to rent on or very near to campus which is great! They are pretty reasonably priced as well.

Q Housing Options Are OK, but Parking ... Not So Much
There is ample off-campus housing, both immediately surrounding the campus and within short distances from the campus.   Parking on and around the Brown University campus is a NIGHTMARE, so most students do not bring cars to school.   So, you tend to see students opt for housing that immediately surrounds the campus so they can still walk or ride bikes to class, etc   Of course, the demand on housing surrounding the campus tends to bring rental costs up, so it is not uncommon to have multiple students sharing a place.

Q Many juniors and seniors live in off-campus housing. There seems to be enough to go around, and it's pretty nice, pretty affordable, and very convenient and close to campus. The campus is very compact, so nothing is a very far walk.

Q It's definitely easy to get. I know a lot of people who live off campus and love it.

Q I couldn't say what it's like, but from my experience walking to off-campus housing, it can be far away from campus. It seems worth it, though, if you want to live in a house and don't want to deal with the housing lottery.

Q Brown doesn't offer off-campus housing until junior year, unless, of course, you call the Office of Student Life and argue. The University tries to keep you on campus as long as it can, which is really quite convenient, since their room and board plan costs considerably more than living and eating in a real apartment in Providence.

The College Prowler Take On...
Off-Campus Housing

Brown guarantees housing for all four years, even though most students opt to live on their own by senior year to gain more freedom, more space, or better facilities. Some years, the University lets juniors live off campus too, but officially, only seniors are guaranteed permission. Students apply to the Office of Residential Life for off-campus permission in the early spring of their junior year, most having already signed a lease in the previous months. As a senior, getting permission is easy, but finding the perfect apartment can be a greater challenge. Within a mile radius of campus there are endless housing options, but the best places are rarely advertised. Hit the pavement or ask friends if you want to find the best place. In general, students can find any kind of place they want—historic houses, new apartments, studios, or mansions.

While most students believe they save money by moving off campus, the frustrations and complications often add up quickly. Summer subletting can be hard, and don't forget the astronomical heating bills during the long winter. Moving off campus should be a careful choice. Since the University requires students to live on campus for a few years, it's easy to know if moving away from the University bubble is right for you.

The College Prowler® Grade on

Off-Campus Housing: C-

A high grade in Off-Campus Housing indicates that apartments are of high quality, close to campus, affordable, and easy to secure.

Diversity

The Lowdown On...
Diversity

African American
6%

Native American
1%

Asian American
15%

White
45%

Hispanic
8%

Unknown
16%

International
8%

Out-of-State Students
96%

Faculty Diversity

African American: 3%
Asian American: 9%
Hispanic: 4%
International: 15%
Native American: 0%
White: 68%
Unknown: 1%

Historically Black College/University?

No

Student Age Breakdown

Under 18: 2%
18-19: 35%
20-21: 33%
22-24: 13%
25+: 18%

Economic Status

Brown recently made a major admissions policy change to accept students on a "need-blind" bases in order to promote quality of scholarship and demonstrated ability above affluence. However, the average Brown student comes from the upper-middle class.

Gay Pride

Brown students and faculty are extremely receptive and friendly to all people, and there have been very few incidences of discrimination or hate crimes related to sexual orientation. The effort to promote queer politics and acceptance is spearheaded by the Queer Alliance. Twice a year, the organization hosts a huge dance that is among the most popular campus parties.

Most Common Religions

Brown does not have a single predominant religion, and the majority of students claim to have no particular affiliation. However, sources show that some religious minorities have particularly high numbers at Brown. Services are provided for students of all religions; they list Bahat, Buddhism, Christianity, Hinduism, Islam, Jainism, Judaism, and Sikhism as the most popular Brown faiths.

Political Activity

The majority of Brown students are very politically active. Many student groups form with a political focus, and acts to raise awareness for issues are commonplace in day-to-day life. Generally, the student body seems to lean more left. Although there is a small and vocal conservative voice, they are a clear minority. Even so, it is fully possible to go about life normally without any political involvement.

Minority Clubs on Campus

The Third World Center at Brown was created in 1976 to meet the needs of all minority students and promote racial and ethnic pluralism in the Brown community. Minority students receive a great deal of support from the Third World Transition Program: the presence of Minority Peer Councelors in freshmen dorms, student publications such as the African Sun and Somos, and program houses such as Harambee House. There are also plenty student organizations for a number of minority groups and their subsets.

Students Speak Out On...
Diversity

ℚ A Very Diverse School!
Brown is an amazingly diverse campus! There are students from all over the world here, and there are many international students, which adds an interesting perspective to the university.

ℚ Could Be Better
There is diversity when it comes to student's backgrounds but not a big diversity on economic backgrounds or personalities. Not a big sexual orientation diversity either but very accepting of none heterosexuals.

ℚ Fake Diversity
Pepople look diverse on the outside, but really people are very similar in the inside. I wish there was more (deeper, more meaningful) diversity, not just black and white, rich and poor.

ℚ The campus is somewhat diverse. There are a lot of people of Asian decent, but other races and ethnicities are underrepresented.

ℚ I feel that Brown is the most diverse of all the Ivys.

ℚ There are people at Brown from all around the world and from all different walks of life, but you might not realize it unless you make an honest effort to get to know people outside your easy social circle. Once you do, however, you end up meeting some pretty awesome people!

Q Diverse compared to what? Compared to Berkeley, it's not diverse. Compared to Princeton, it's very diverse. I don't know; people have different opinions on this, too.

Q It's not terrible. We're doing okay by the percentages. But it's very hard to be here and forget that you are in very white, very middle-class New England. I don't think it's an us-versus-them environment, but the manifestation of relations, either racial or class, exist.

The College Prowler Take On...
Diversity

Brown makes an honest effort to promote socioeconomic diversity in the student body—the recent change to need-blind admissions is just one example of this goal. Also, a large endowment several years ago (the biggest single gift ever made to Brown) promises to preserve the goal of providing financial aid to deserving students. While the hard numbers indicate that there is a good deal of racial and economic diversity at Brown, the day-to-day interactions between students are the real test of diversity and tolerance at Brown. There a very few outright problems or public sentiments that indicate a lack of diversity at Brown. In spite of this, students do not necessarily integrate themselves in their social circles.

The University gives Brown the basic ingredients to enjoy diversity in political, economic, racial, and geographical areas. It also provides support for students who come from a variety of backgrounds. Regardless of background, every student will be in a situation where they are confronted with people and opinions that they have never experienced before coming here. The vocal nature of Brown students and the University's outstanding policies, which protect freedom of student expression, mean that the school is as diverse as the students here make it.

A-

The College Prowler® Grade on

Diversity: A-

A high grade in Diversity indicates that ethnic minorities and international students have a notable presence on campus and that students of different economic backgrounds, religious beliefs, and sexual preferences are well-represented.

Guys & Girls

The Lowdown On...
Guys & Girls

Female Undergrads
53%

Male Undergrads
47%

Birth Control Available?

Yes: Residential counselors and health services make contraceptives readily available to students.

Social Scene

Brown students generally can be put into two groups: social butterflies and social caterpillars. It makes for a great dynamic. Just when you think you've exhausted your social sphere, you meet someone in a class who, it turns out, lived down the hall from you for two years but never left their room. That being said, freshmen housing units are the basis for future social interaction at Brown. In freshmen units, personalities spill into the hallways and start friendships that may last a lifetime. At Brown, a smile really is all it takes to meet people.

Hookups or Relationships?

Very few students seem to carry deep, long-term relationships, but a good number of them do exist. However, Brown is a school where hookups reign supreme. Most students would say they are simply too busy and too involved to pursue a committed relationship. Brown also seems to attract many freshmen with little or no relationship experience. It's impossible to say what combination of factors lead to the two most common sentiments about Brown students and dating: "there is no dating at Brown," and "we're just friends with benefits."

Dress Code

The dressing tendencies at Brown tend to be all over the place. The majority of students dress like you would expect any other college students to dress. You will definitely see your share of designer clothing and hip style and fashion here. Particularly in the winter, fashion seems to give way to functionality, but even then, students manage to show off some personal flair. Conversely, a good number of students seem to just throw together whatever isn't in the laundry. Overall, there is a broad spectrum of dressing, so regardless of your own personal style, chances are you'll feel comfortable with how you dress.

Did You Know?

Top Three Places to Find Hotties:
1. Thayer Street, Max's, and Viva
2. Wriston Quad
3. The Main Green

Top Five Places to Hook Up:
1. The 12th floor of the Sci-Li
2. The Underground
3. The GCB
4. A freshmen lounge
5. The Main Green

Students Speak Out On...
Guys & Girls

ℚ Brunonians Are Lovely!
People at Brown seem to be either single or in a long-term relationship. I'm not entirely sure how that happens. People at Brown are fantastic in general!!

ℚ A Beautiful Rainbow
The typical student looks very comfortable. Everyone has their own distinct style, so there isn't an overwhelming need to fit in. The social life is always vibrant, there is always something going on. Interests vary, depending on lifestyles, gender, and where people are from. The relationships in the academic environment are respectful and always a learning experience.

ℚ Lots of Cliques
The guys and girls at Brown tend to be quite cliquey; the pre-meds, artsy types, rich kids, and jocks tend not to intermix. The group that sticks out the most, though, is the athletes. Not only do they have an entirely different physique and level of physical attractiveness than all of the other students (partially due to the lower academic standard in the recruitment process), but they tend to adopt a "party" lifestyle, and tend to be markedly more politically conservative than the uber-liberals at Brown.

ℚ
I'd have to say the guys at Brown are hotter than the girls. It's not exactly a big dating school, but people do date and hook up.

ℚ
Beautiful women. So many beautiful women.

Q If you're not the type who can say, "I like her for her personality, not her looks," and mean it, don't go to Brown.

Q The guys here are okay. Considering it is an Ivy League school, the boys here a pretty inexperienced, but there is definitely a lot of sex going around on weekends. Girls at Brown tend to be more attractive than the guys. Sad, I know.

Q I don't think the students at Brown are significantly more or less attractive on average than any other school. There is no typical student, really.

The College Prowler Take On...
Guys & Girls

According to the rumors, the headshots Brown requires with every application are meant to ensure Brown's reputation for having the most attractive Ivy League students. Whether or not you believe this rumor is entirely a matter of taste (and whether you consider "attractive Ivy League student" an oxymoron). In general, students tend to agree that the admissions office does a fabulous job choosing interesting and enjoyable classmates, but they are a little more critical when it comes to sharing anything more than intellectual curiosity with their peers. However, the truth of the matter is that the Brown student body is no more or less attractive than any other population of 20-year-old students; observers are just as likely to rave about the spectacular beauties lounging on the Main Green as they are to complain about the pale, four-eyed creatures that wander out of the library late at night.

The only real consensus is on the state of the dating scene: There isn't one. Students chose between serial relationships, random hookups, or celibacy. While this is a common complaint on Friday nights, the system is probably perpetuated because it suits the busy Brown lifestyle.

Guys: B

The College Prowler®
Grade on

Guys & Girls

A high grade for Guys or Girls indicates that the students on campus is attractive, smart, friendly, and engaging, and that the school has a decent gender ratio.

Girls: B

www.collegeprowler.com

Athletics

The Lowdown On...
Athletics

Athletic Association
NAA
NCAA

Athletic Division
NCAA Division I-AA

Athletic Conferences
Football: Ivy Group
Basketball: Ivy Group

School Colors
Brown, red, and white

School Nickname/ Mascot
The Brown Bear

Men Playing Varsity Sports
511: 18%

Women Playing Varsity Sports
477: 16%

Men's Varsity Sports

Baseball
Basketball
Fencing
Football
Golf
Ice hockey
Lacrosse
Rowing
Soccer
Squash
Swimming and diving
Tennis
Track and field
Water polo
Wrestling

Women's Varsity Sports

Basketball
Equestrian
Fencing
Field hockey
Golf
Gymnastics
Ice hockey
Lacrosse
Rowing
Skiing
Soccer
Softball
Squash
Swimming and diving
Tennis
Track and field
Volleyball
Water polo

Intramurals

Badminton
Basketball
Basketball golf
Dodgeball
Flag football
Golf
Ice hockey
Kickball
Soccer
Softball
Squash
Tennis
Trivia bowl
Ultimate Frisbee
Volleyball
Wiffleball

Club Sports

Field hockey
Ice hockey
Lacrosse (men's, women's)
Rugby (men's, women's)
Sailing
Skiing
Soccer (men's, women's)
Tennis (men's, women's)
Ultimate Frisbee (men's, women's)
Volleyball (men's)

Athletic Fields & Facilities

Bear's Lair Athletic Center
Hunter S. Marston Boathouse
Meehan Auditorium Ice Rink
Olney-Margolies Athletic Center (OMAC)

Pembroke Field
Pizzitola Sports Center
Smith Swim Center

Most Popular Sports

The most popular sport on campus, in terms of participation, seems to be ultimate Frisbee. Overall, varsity sports tend to receive rather weak spectatorship.

Most Overlooked Teams

Although the equestrian team is ranked among the best in the nation, it rarely seems to get support or recognition.

School Spirit

Brunonians are generally very proud of their school, in all aspects. Though support for athletics is not particularly strong, students, faculty, and alumni are quick to support and recognize any accomplishment made by the school or its people.

Getting Tickets

Since most varsity athletic events are only moderately attended, it is only hard to get tickets for the biggest games of the year. In most cases, showing up to an event with your Brown ID is all you need to get in. For information, call (401) 863-2773.

Best Place to Take a Walk

For a casual stroll, there's plenty of exploring to be done just by walking the streets around campus. If you're up for a workout, a run downtown and back will give you good hill climbing training.

Students Speak Out On...
Athletics

Q Top-Notch Sailing Team - Bravo!

Brown University has a fantastic sailing team - consistently among the top ten in the country for both coed and womens, despite it's 'club varsity' status

Q School Spirit

Many Brown students enjoy going to athletic events and games, but sports culture is not that big on campus. The athletes usually stick with other athletes. I personally haven't been to any sports related events yet at Brown.

Q I Wish We Had More Team Spirit

I'm not an athlete, but I do like to go to certain sports games. Sometimes I find myself wishing the I went to a school that supported their teams more. Also, the satellite athletic facilities could use more machines.

Q No One Cares

Brown is not known for our sports - therefore no one really cares. Don't get me wrong, some of our teams are nationally ranked, so we do have good sports.

Q

Varsity sports are definitely present, and they're a good program if that's your thing. Intramurals are so much fun, and a lot of kids get into basketball, football, softball, and Frisbee.

Q

Intramurals are pretty popular. Varsity sports are almost like a social scene, and like all other social scenes, it's fractious and segregated from most other things. Part of the reason is that there's less of a stigma for athletes; it's more that the sports complex is not physically in the center of campus.

Q Club sports are a lot of fun without the pressure of varsity sports. There's a huge culture that revolves around the ultimate Frisbee teams. I play club ultimate Frisbee. There's no varsity team, but the club team travels a lot.

Q What's a varsity sport? No, seriously, if you're looking for colleges where you can be a celebrity on campus because you are an athlete, then look elsewhere. My friends that are varsity athletes work very hard, and it is difficult for them to have social lives outside of their teams. Some of them end up dropping the team; others have a great experience so they stick with it and love their teammates and their sport.

The College Prowler Take On...
Athletics

Brown is not an overly athletic school. Almost every student played some varsity sport in high school, but for most students, academics and other extracurricular activities come before athletics. However, there are a full range of varsity sports and less-intense club and intramural sports. Many Brown students go for runs around campus, or they find themselves playing catch or Frisbee on the Main Green.

Sports are just one aspect of social life, and they help relieve stress from the academic rigors of the University. Brown has facilities for non-athletes to swim, work out, and play organized sports. Brown also has gifted student athletes who may go underappreciated despite winning records.

B-

The College Prowler® Grade on

Athletics: B-

A high grade in Athletics indicates that students have school spirit, that sports programs are respected, that games are well-attended, and that intramurals are a prominent part of student life.

Nightlife

The Lowdown On...
Nightlife

Cheapest Place to Get a Drink
Grad Center Bar
The Red Fez

Primary Areas with Nightlife
Downtown Providence

Closing Time
1 a.m. on weeknights
2 a.m. on weekends

Useful Resources for Nightlife
www.brown.dailyjolt.com

Club Listings

Club Hell

73 Richmond St.
Providence
(401) 351-1977
www.club-hell.com
Club Hell hosts the retro
and fetish club scene in
Providence. Although it's
no closer than any other
downtown night spot, Hell
attracts a good number
of Brown students, and
maintains a good balance
of edgy and accessible.
Cover ranges from $4 to
$6 Tuesday: Underground
eighties, Hell's busiest
night. Bust a move or bang
heads to the Ramones, the
Cramps, Bowie, and their
contemporaries. Sunday:
Resurrection, Providence's
goth night.

The Complex

180 Pine St.
Downtown
(401) 751-4263
www.thecomplexri.com
A Providence dance staple,
the Complex promises to suit
almost any taste in its boring,
yet crowd pleasing, ways.
ladies night and college night
keep the students coming,
and the meager five-dollar
cover gets them in and
dancing. Casual dress, casual
looks, and casual interaction.
It's unlikely that you'll run

into many other Brown kids,
but sometimes that's a good
thing. If you are looking to
cut loose Thursday–Saturday,
the Complex is a safe bet.
Thursday–Saturday $5 cover.

Fish Company

515 South Water St.
Providence
(401) 421-5796
Despite the admittedly
disgusting name, the Fish
Company is not a packing
house by day turned club at
night (although that might
give it a bit more mystique).
This is a club that Brown kids
frequent, most likely because
it's close to campus and easy
to find. Drinks might not be
cheap enough, considering
the very casual atmosphere,
but at least you can get
fresh air on the deck, which
has a nice view of the river.
Wednesday: Live Music.
Thursday–Saturday: DJ.

Lupo's at the Strand

70 Washington St.
Providence
(401) 245-9840
www.lupos.com
The granddaddy of
Providence nightlife, Lupo's
is a world-famous concert
venue, bar, and occasional
dance floor. A great place
to catch soon-to-be-huge
bands, Lupo's consistently

pleases with a perfect lineup of hot bands, has-beens, and second-rate groups ranging from hip-hop and reggae to indie rock and ska. The Met Café, Lupo's sibling club, promises smaller, intimate shows with a full bar right next door.

Metropolis
127 Friendship St.
Providence
(401) 454-5483
Metropolis promises to be a hard-hitting club. Metropolis lives up to its name with multiple dance floors and spinning DJs. Grab your trendiest gear and a crisp Hamilton; ten bucks gets you in this big-city dance club. It tries hard to mimic the New York club feel, but it's only open Thursday–Saturday.

Pulse
86 Crary St.
Downtown
(401) 272-2133
Go-go boys and sweat-drenched bodies are the fare at Pulse, one of Rhode Island's largest gay clubs. Features all-male reviews. Thursday: Karaoke with denise. No cover before 10. Friday: Hetero-a-Go-Go. All persuasions welcome.

Viva
234 Thayer St.
Middle of campus
(401) 331-6200
Viva has been on campus for 10 years, and based on the line to get in on Saturday nights, it's not leaving any time soon. There's no denying that Viva found its clientele in Brown's club-hungry international students. From the looks of it, you'll think you walked into a wormhole and were instantly transported to a glamorous city. Strong drinks, thick smoke, and even thicker accents are the scene. It's a see-and-be-seen hotspot. And don't even think about wearing those sneakers. Open seven nights a week with a variable cover.

Bar Listings
Grad Center Bar
90 Thayer St.
On campus
(401) 421-0270
Nothing says get sauced like cheap drinks, cheap pool, and a bar that opens at four in the afternoon. The GCB is a great place for students to share a pitcher with their professors, TAs, or classmates. Unfortunately for most underclassmen,

they are serious about IDs. Memberships to the GCB can be purchased with $20, a Brown ID, and driver's license.

Kartabar

284 Thayer St.
Providence
(401) 331-8111
www.kartabar.com
Popular for its boutique-chic atmosphere and its signature drinks, Kartabar is another stop along the Thayer Street bar scene. Students have strong drinks and see bafflingly overdressed patrons sip martinis and snack on European appetizers.

Liquid Lounge

165 Angell St.
On campus
(401) 621-8752
Smack in the middle of campus, Liquid Lounge's neon lights call to Brown students looking for a chill bar experience. Here the local and college crowd mix like oil and water, but everyone can get hosed together on dollar Rolling Rocks while listening to a rocking juke box.

Nick-a-Nees

76 South St.
Providence

(401) 861-7290
Although it's a little out of the way, Brown students occasionally pack its long tables, which are inevitably laden with peanut shells and the occasional broken glass. It's not much to look at, but Brown students dig dive bars, and Nick-a-Nees has dived about as far as it can go. Sometimes friendly staff, cheap eats, and live blues and rock bands make the bar a welcomed change from the packed college bars only a few miles away.

Patrick's Pub

381 Smith St.
Providence
(401) 751-1553
Patrick's has become something of a Providence staple, if not to Brown students in particular. Saturday night is college night, cover is $2 instead of $5 if you wear green.

The Red Fez

49 Peck St.
Providence
(401) 272-1212
Another wonderful dive bar, the Red Fez features a short bar and church-pew-style seating that makes you wonder if you've found the last-bastion for nerd glasses and MC5 T-shirts. Regardless,

a semi-cold can of Schlitz for a buck and a half is enough to lure Brown hipsters downtown for a drink where nobody knows your name.

Steam Alley
520 S. Water St.
Providence
(401) 751-1820
Steam Alley is just a few blocks farther than most Brown students wander, but is less than a block from the ever-popular Fish Company. This relaxing bar has multiple big-screen TVs, cheap pool tables, and karaoke.

Tortilla Flats
355 Hope St.
Providence
(401) 751-6777
www.tortillaflatsri.com
Only a few blocks form Brown's campus, Tortilla Flats may seem like a godsend for anyone who notices the conspicuous lack of Mexican food around campus. Sadly, nada mucho here, as far as food goes. The extensive line-up of tequila bottles, however, will leave you spinning like a piñata on Cinco de Mayo.

Trinity Brewhouse
186 Fountain St.
Providence
(401) 453-2337

www.trinitybrewhouse.com
A downtown microbrew, Trinity Brewhouse features patio seating in the heart of downtown. On Tuesdays, you can get a scenic tour of the facility, but the bar is a great place to grab a pint any day of the week.

Wickenden Pub
320 Wickenden St.
Providence
(401) 861-2555
The Wick Pub is close to a lot of off-campus housing. The drinks aren't cheap, but if you want to feel like you're drinking in the hull of a ship, they've got you covered. The pub showcases over 100 different bottles of beer in their front window, and you can join the Pint Club by drinking all of them.

The Wild Colonial Tavern
250 S. Water St.
Providence
(401) 621-5644
Voted one of the 50 best bars in America, the Wild Colonial is run by Brown professors. Pints of Guinness and darts abound at the foot of College Hill.

Favorite Drinking Games

Beirut/beer pong
Card games (A$$hole, Kings)
Power Hour
Quarters

What to Do if You're Not 21

Trinity Repertory

201 Washington St.
Providence
(401) 351-4242
Trinity Reparatory Company performs first-class theater performances produced by its own resident acting company. They features classics as well as contemporary works by local, national, and international playwrites, and it has special offers.

Underground AS220

121 Empire St.
Downtown
(401) 861-9190
Although it's a bar, AS220 is always all-ages and drinking really is only part of the scene.

Organization Parties

A number of student organizations regularly throw parties at a variety of locations. Most of these are open to anyone who wants to come, even those not affiliated with the organization. Quite often multiple organizations will team together to increase turnout and resources.

Students Speak Out On...
Nightlife

Q House Parties Are the Thing
Overall, there is lots to do both on & off campus, from shows to movies to bars to parties.   But, most students tend to attend house/dorm parties, where they can walk back to their room later.

Q Thayer
Thayer is the main street and there are a few bars/clubs during the weeknights and weekends. The greek life has a few major parties each semester, but isn't the main source of entertainment.

Q
Parties on campus range widely and are widely dispersed. The frats are definitely not the main places to go for parties, unless that's your scene.

Q
There are some great bars around town. I love Patrick's. I used to go to there by myself on Saturday mornings to watch soccer. It would be 10 a.m. on a Saturday, and it would be me, the bartender, and an 80-year-old man. I would ask for breakfast, and the bartender would offer me a beer with it.

Q
I'm not a fan of drinking, therefore the parties for me aren't fun.

Q
Parties on campus are alright. The frat parties get old after awhile. Machado House holds the best parties. There's a nearby club called Fish Co. that is a real hot spot—Wednesday is Brown college night. Of course, Brown's two biggest controversial parties are SexPowerGod

and Starf*ck. There's an awesome gay club in downtown Providence called Mirabar. Here, workers can be found walking around the dance floor with jello tube shots in hand and wearing nothing but tighty whities and sneakers.

Q Parties tend to be either large dance parties in fraternities or small spontaneous events with friends in dorm rooms. Both are fun but can get repetitive and boring after a while.

Q The parties are lame. Wriston, the quad where the frats are, is really often the only option unless you are part of student groups whose upperclass members throw house parties. If you are into clubs, lots of kids go to Fish Co. on Wednesday nights, but it seems like a huge bro/female-degrading fest.

The College Prowler Take On...
Nightlife

Brown students are more fond of bars than clubs. However, if you really need to party every night, Providence has a few dozen clubs that will expose you to Rhode Island nightlife, which can be gritty but holds promise for hot people and decent tunes. If drinking is all you need, Providence's bars, like its restaurants, cater to all styles and tastes.

Although Brown students are not the most adventurous, the bars, clubs, and other nightlife activities lurking in the city can entertain the blandest or wildest tastes any night of the week. Every day, bars are swinging on College Hill, downtown, and everywhere else in the city until at least 1 in the morning. Brown students who think that there's not enough to do after the sun goes down need to open their eyes, expand their bubble, and venture out to one of Providence's eager-to-please nightspots.

The College Prowler® Grade on
Nightlife: B+

A high grade in Nightlife indicates that there are many bars and clubs in the area that are easily accessible and affordable. Other determining factors include the number of options for the under-21 crowd and the prevalence of house parties.

Greek Life

The Lowdown On...
Greek Life

Undergrad Men in Fraternities
10%

Number of Sororities
2

Undergrad Women in Sororities
7%

Number of Fraternities
6

Fraternities
Alpha Epsilon Pi
Delta Phi
Delta Tau
Phi Kappa Psi
Sigma Chi
Theta Delta Chi

Sororities
Alpha Chi Omega
Kappa Alpha Theta

Multicultural Colonies
Alpha Delta Phi
Zeta Delta Xi

Other Greek Organizations
Alpha Delta Phi
Greek Council
Greek Peer Advisors
Interfraternity Council
Order of Omega
Panhellenic Council
Zeta Delta Xi (co-ed
fraternity)

Students Speak Out On...
Greek Life

Q Exists, but Not Huge
There are several frats, but they're a pretty small part of campus life.

Q Greeks Aren't Huge
Greek life at Brown is not huge. Those who belong to the Greek life enjoy it and get to know each other and take advantage of the perks. For those who don't it is not a big deal, since it is a small deal, most social events do not revolve around it.

Q
I lived in Bodega House, the creative expression house, which is not Greek life. It was a program house sandwiched between a normal frat and non-affiliated residents. Brown put a revolving door between our space and the frat's, and right away we felt physically separated. To counter the sense of separation, we had residential programmers who planned activities for the people in the building.

Q
Some people are in frats and sororities, and there are frat parties. It's not very big, though. It's like being in another club or program house, but the name is Greek. It's no big deal—it's not a matter of popularity or status.

Q
There's definitely a Greek presence, and it's a source of parties, but I've personally never been to one, and that's not a big deal. There's really no pressure either way.

Q It's about 10 percent of housing, I guess, and frat parties are about 50 percent of the party scene. Some frats, like King House, are kind of dorky and cute. The only traditional frat is Sigma Kai, and it throws good parties.

Q I don't know anything about Greek life at Brown.

Q Greek life is definitely there, but it in no way dominates the social scene. They have a lot of the parties on campus, that can be fun, but it is definitely avoidable and not seen as being a big deal at all.

The College Prowler Take On...
Greek Life

Greek life at Brown is about as minimal as it can be. This is due to the Greek system itself and the University's attempts to seamlessly integrate frats and sororities into daily campus life. All Greek houses are on campus and abide by the same rules and regulations as any other organization on campus. The parties, for the most part, are open and welcoming to all students. If students never want to see the Greek system, they can easily ignore it. On the flip side, if students want a real Greek experience, they can find it in one of the dozen houses that exist.

The Greek system at Brown is one of the many positive interest groups. Banners hang around the Main Green and Wriston Quad to inform students of coming parties and events. A handful of nights during the year, you see the crazy, Animal House-type antics that Greek systems present at any school. However, if you want a school where you are defined by the three Greek letters printed on your T-shirt, Brown is simply not the place.

The College Prowler® Grade on
Greek Life: C-

A high grade in Greek Life indicates that sororities and fraternities are not only present, but also active on campus. Other determining factors include the variety of houses available and the respect the Greek community receives from the rest of the campus.

Drug Scene

The Lowdown On...
Drug Scene

Most Popular Drugs
Alcohol
Cocaine
Marijuana
Speed
Study drugs

**Alcohol-Related
Referrals**
28

**Alcohol-Related
Arrests**
0

Drug-Related Referrals
29

Drug-Related Arrests
1

Drug Counseling Programs
Health Service
3rd floor of health services
(401) 863-2794
Provide information concerning substance abuse issues,
counseling

Students Speak Out On...
Drug Scene

Q Not huge, but it definitely exists
The drug scene at Brown is really whatever you make it to be. If you are interested in drugs, then it is relatively easy to find them and others who feel the same way. Likewise, if it's something you want to avoid, then it's easy to do this too.Alcohol is big here, like at any college. There's usually enough stuff going on around campus during the weekend to easily find events without alcohol, though.I haven't been to any other colleges to compare, but I would say that the pot scene here is bigger than at most colleges. Most people just smoke in their rooms, so it's easy to avoid it if you want to. Acid and mushrooms are not common overall, but they are pretty popular among the stoners and hardcore potheads. If you don't hang out with these people, then you're probably never going to see these drugs.

Q Drinking Is More Popular
Drugs are definitely here, but not out in the open. People smoke pot, but even that isn't too blatant. Drinking is very prevalent, but you need to seek out drugs to be able to do them.

Q Drugs at Brown
The drug scene at Brown varies. For those interested, there are places where you can find them and people who want to participate. For those who don't, it will never be hard to find events without drugs.

Q Not Really

As far as I have seen, drugs aren't a big scene at Brown. What's more prevalent is alcohol and marijuana. People get drunk and high a lot. Drugged, not so much.

Q Yeah, most of my friends smoke and drink. I wouldn't date someone who doesn't smoke or drink, I think it's like that at most universities. I have friends outside of that group that I meet in class or at work to get a cup of coffee with, but people kind of stick to their circles here.

Q If you want to find the scene, you can find it pretty quickly. If you don't want to, you can stay away from it. People are pretty open about their personal habits.

Q Pot is the most used and accessible illicit drug at Brown. However, coke, acid, mushrooms, and ecstasy also seem to be around from time to time. The scene is avoidable if you so choose. I haven't really heard anything about heroin, which is a good thing.

Q I would say most students do drink, but not a lot. I would say the average student would, at most, have four drinks—I mean in a night, not in an hour.

The College Prowler Take On...
Drug Scene

While you can guarantee some exposure to drugs, it is by no means a social prerequisite. There is enough to do at Brown and in Providence to stave off the boredom that makes the drug scene thrive at other less-entertaining schools. Brown students, like any college student body, look to drugs for both social and academic reasons. Many students drink and smoke cigarettes and pot casually. From there, the scenes are more obscure and are neither prominent nor hard to find. Students at Brown tend to view substance use as a luxury that can be enjoyed with personal responsibility. The effects that abuse will have on your work and the threat of University and police action if you get caught keep students using drugs sensibly on campus.

In the end, students are neither excluded nor included socially based purely on their drug habits, and Brown students exhibit the full spectrum of personal habits. The most important thing to remember is that most Brown students are responsible and goal-driven kids. Drug use is more a byproduct of college life than a main activity.

B

The College Prowler® Grade on

Drug Scene: B

A high grade in the Drug Scene indicates that drugs are not a noticeable part of campus life; drug use is not visible, and no pressure to use them seems to exist.

Campus Strictness

The Lowdown On...
Campus Strictness

Students Are Most Likely to Get Caught...
Smoking cigarettes in the dorms.
Smoking pot in the dorms.

Students Speak Out On...
Campus Strictness

Q None
Not strict at all. No police arrests, no trouble, no adults watching over you.

Q Not Strict
Brown is not strict whatsoever. There is plenty of underage drinking and people are very rarely busted for it. On weekends, most of the parties are at the frat houses on Wriston Quad, and there is plenty of visible underage drinking, but you are unlikely to get in trouble for this. The campus is also not strict about pot at all. However, if you do this outside, then you are more likely to get caught. Most people just smoke in their rooms, and the chances of getting caught for this are practically zero. Also, unlike many other schools, the RA's here do not write up students or take away alcohol. They are there to give students advice and help students make good decisions. Overall, the school seems to be more interested in helping students make the right decisions rather than getting students in trouble.

Q Moderate Strictness
Most often, campus police monitor parties and exceptionally unruly behavior and don't interfere with students' usual activities.

Q Police generally don't look for people doing stuff. But it's not like they'll pretend they didn't see it if they happen to come upon it.

Q I don't know the exact rules, but I always feel safe. Parties rarely get busted.

Q It's not strict. Room inspections are so lenient, and everything is pretty lax—except for the parking enforcement who are good at their jobs.

Q It's pretty inconsistent. You won't get in serious trouble with campus police, but be careful about your roommates, counselors, and other neighbors. It's probably not a good idea to throw a kegger in your room.

Q You have to try pretty hard to get in trouble here. The only dean's hearing I've gotten was for partying on the roof. We didn't get in trouble for the smoking and drinking, so much as being on the roof. Just use a little common sense, and you'll be fine.

The College Prowler Take On...
Campus Strictness

The Brown police are not unlike those cool parents you knew in high school: They let the kids have their parties and almost never check out suspicious smells. While the police will nab students for any blatant displays of illegal behavior, they are unlikely to look for it unless staff or students notify them. These days, the main job of the Brown police is crime prevention and not student supervision. In addition, the counselor support system in the dorms provides a safe, open, and fun environment for the students, not a tool for the University to keep an eye on the students in their rooms.

Although many people think enforcement is lax, people do go to dean's hearings and letters of reprimand are issued every time. The first few offenses stay confidential, but if the school is aware of a real problem, they will notify your parents and require counseling for social- and substance-related issues. Blatant acts of crime against other students, on the other hand, are dealt with more harshly. The University establishes safe, yet liberal boundaries for students and uses security presence to protect, not police, the students.

The College Prowler® Grade on

Campus
Strictness: A-

A high Campus Strictness grade implies an overall lenient atmosphere; police and RAs are fairly tolerant, and the administration's rules are flexible.

Parking

The Lowdown On...
Parking

Parking Services
Brown University Police and Security
75 Charleslfield St.
(401) 863-3157

Approximate Parking Permit Cost
$720 per year

Student Parking Lot
Yes

Freshmen Allowed to Park
No

Common Parking Tickets
Brown lots without a permit: $25-$75
Expired meter: $10
Handicapped zone: $50
No parking zone: $15

Getting a Parking Permit
Permits and spaces are handed out through a seniority basis lottery. The lottery is held the second Monday of April for spaces to be given out the following year. Freshmen who bring cars to campus are not given access to the official Brown parking system. Keeping a car is not really feasible for any student, and most will find that it is not necessary.

Did You Know?

Best Places to Find a Parking Spot
There are a few good secret spots in alleys or on un-metered streets, and if you are patient, you can circle the campus a few times and usually find something. The meters are poorly placed and usually broken, so the odds of getting a completely free space are good, but you will have to move your car every two hours. As you get farther from campus, the time limits become more liberal, the spaces more plentiful, and the odds of getting ticketed much lower.

Good Luck Getting a Parking Spot Here
On a rainy or snowy day, don't even think about trying to drive in and find a spot around campus or on Thayer. On most days, however, the two-hour parking limit keeps cars shuffling and makes the dismal prospect of finding a spot evenly difficult anywhere around campus.

Students Speak Out On...
Parking

Q Parking Sucks
Parking is terrible, except if you live off-campus a lot of houses come with parking spaces

Q Pretty Bad
I'm only a freshman at Brown, but I work at the info desk. So, I often have to direct visitors around campus. The main parking lot is often full. Being situated in a medium sized city, Brown is a somewhat condensded campus. It is very hard to find a spot at times. Only juniors and seniors are allowed to have parking permits.

Q Parking la Hard to Find!
Parking is only really available for seniors. You can purchase spots off campus as an underclassman but they are very expensive.

Q Practically Nonexistant
There is essentially no parking. First and second year students can't even have cars, and most upper class students don't because even if you can get a place to park near your dorm/apartment, there's nowhere to park near class.

Q
Fortunately, I have always been able to get on-campus parking or parking through local landlords who rent out a space for a semester. But if that doesn't work out, the Brown shuttle is great for taking you anywhere around campus. It runs pretty frequently—maybe every 10 minutes or so. There are also trolleys that can take you downtown to the mall, bars, clubs, and restaurants.

Q Don't bring a car. Parking is not the greatest, but you don't need a car because everything is walkable.

Q Parking is difficult but possible! After freshman year, you can enter the parking lottery and get a reserved spot for the following year.

Q It is not easy to park if you are a freshman. In fact, you are not allowed to have a car the first semester, so the people who do end up moving their cars to different places early in the morning. However, it really is not necessary to have a car. Basically everything is within walking distance, and Providence has a very good trolley system that takes you around for 50 cents. The campus is also a 15-minute walk from the train station, which has very cheap commuter trains to Boston. And the bus station is about a 10-minute walk away. Transportation is really convenient.

The College Prowler Take On...
Parking

Do you like your car? Do you have a financial or emotional incentive to keep it in peak condition? Have you become accustomed to convenient and free parking? If you answered "yes" to any of these questions, you might want to seriously reconsider bringing your car to campus. The cruel winters and even crueler parking cops make street parking a dangerous proposition. If a snowplow doesn't hit your car, a $10 ticket will. It's widely known that the Providence city government is funded largely on parking tickets. Having a car, therefore, will probably cost you another $50 a month in parking tickets. It's not as bad as the big cities, but you will start to get frustrated with the little orange friends you find on your windshield.

Brown parking also leaves a lot to be desired. Upperclassmen are usually able to get a university parking spot in a safe, covered lot, but there are far fewer good spots than students who want them. Most underclassmen are forced to park in a lot that's so far away it is only accessible by car. Private parking lots are the most popular choice for students, but they come at a high cost. Most students choose not to bring a car until senior year when they can park at an off-campus house or get a good university parking spot.

C+

The College Prowler® Grade on
Parking: C+

A high grade in the Parking section indicates that parking is both available and affordable, and that parking enforcement isn't overly severe.

Transportation

The Lowdown On...
Transportation

Best Ways to Get Around Town
Bike
Buses/trolleys
Walk

Campus Shuttle
Brown Escort Service
This service provides transportation between University buildings and off-campus residences that are within the service's boundaries.
(401) 863-1778

Daily 5 p.m.–3 a.m.

Brown Shuttle Service
The shuttle runs a set route around campus with 12 stops and promises no more than a seven-minute wait. Riders must show IDs to board.
Daily 5 p.m.–3 a.m.

BrownMed/Downcity Express
Transportation for Brown/ RISD medical students to local hospitals.

Public Transit
Rhode Island Public Transit Authority (RIPTA)
(401) 781-9400
www.brown.dailyjolt.com/
transportation

Best Ways to Get to the Airport
A cab ride to the airport costs about $30.
The Airport Shuttle - (401) 737-2868 The shuttle runs from Brown's Faunce Arch and picks up students at 27 minutes past the hour, but you should call to confirm they are running on the day you need service.
There is a free shuttle that operates during extended school vacations.

Nearest Airport
T.F. Green Airport (PVD)
(401) 737-4000
www.pvdairport.com
T.F. Green is an international airport located about nine miles from Brown and is approximately a 15-minute drive from campus.

Nearest Passenger Bus
Bonanza
(401) 751-8800
Bonanza Bus service runs out

of both the bus depot off I-95 exit 25 and downtown Kennedy Plaza Bus station

Kennedy Plaza Bus Station
Washington and Dorrance Streets, Downtown

Providence Greyhound , Trailways Bus Terminal
1 Kennedy Plaza, Providence
(401) 454-0790
www.greyhound.com

Nearest Passenger Train
Providence Amtrak Station
100 Gaspee St., Providence
(401) 727-7370
www.amtrak.com

Students Speak Out On...
Transportation

Q Buses Are Decent, Shuttles Are Minimal
We technically have campus shuttles at night, but they run long, inconvenient circuits and most people don't bother using them. The free bus rides on RIPTA are nice, but the buses don't run very late.

Q Campus Is Very Small
there is rarely a need for transportation besides walking

Q Saferide Sucks
SafeRide service does not have much room, and it is more of a van than a shuttle with rude and incompetent drivers.

Q We have free shuttles that are relatively reliable. The only problem is that there's no reason to go anywhere in the area around Brown. Getting to the train station is pretty easy, though.

Q We're within walking distance to the bus or the train.

Q Public transportation is okay. Trolleys, busses, and cabs can get you around the city. However, taxis can be late or stand you up—particularly when you really need them late at night or when you need to get to the airport or train station. Fortunately, on a nice day, everything is in walking distance.

Q Public transportation is very easy. It's everywhere. Anything you need is a mile away, but you generally don't have to trek on foot if you don't want to. There's a trolley

for 50 cents, buses, and a train station. The airport is a 15-minute drive away. There are taxis, student shuttles, and a safety walk. They've got it covered.

Q Transportation is wonderful for getting out of the city to go to New York, Boston, and Newport. There are many trains within walking distance, and they are inexpensive as well. Buses run in and out of the city. To tell you the truth, people rarely use them. Everyone who doesn't have a car pretty much walks everywhere. Everything in downtown Providence is pretty much within walking distance.

The College Prowler Take On...
Transportation

For such a small city, Providence offers a lot of options to travel within the city and to other big cities. If you want to get to New York or Boston via train or bus, you can walk downhill to the station in about 10 minutes. Within the city, trolleys run to major areas of town, and they are cheap and run regularly. There are also a lot of people on campus brave enough to bring cars, so it's easy to bum rides.

Cheap and reliable, Providence's RIPTA system will get you everywhere you need without the hassle of having a car. Many Brown students use public transportation infrequently because most missions can be accomplished without having to leave College Hill, but when you need them, a trolley, bus, or train are waiting to carry you away.

A-

The College Prowler® Grade on

Transportation: A-

A high grade for Transportation indicates that campus buses, public buses, cabs, and rental cars are readily-available and affordable. Other determining factors include proximity to an airport and the necessity of transportation.

Weather

The Lowdown On...
Weather

Temperature Averages
Spring – High: 58 °F
Spring – Low: 39 °F
Summer – High: 80 °F
Summer – Low: 62 °F
Fall – High: 63 °F
Fall – Low: 44 °F
Winter – High: 39 °F
Winter – Low: 23 °F

Precipitation Averages
Spring: 4.08 in.
Summer: 3.48 in.
Fall: 3.93 in.
Winter: 3.99 in.

Students Speak Out On...
Weather

Q All Seasons.

In Providence, you get to see all the seasons. Fall is, to me, the most beautiful - so many warm colors and the climate is just right...it's my favorite. Winter was a bit hard for me (coming from Texas) because THERE'S SO MUCH SNOW. But I got used to it. Just make sure you buy a good winter coat and nice boots and little accessories like scarves, gloves, hats, etc. and you'll be fine. Spring is gorgeous too. Everyone will be outdoors laying on the grass and taking advantage of the weather during springtime. And summer is HOT (but not quite as hot as Texas) and VERY humid (a lot more so than I'm used to). Oh yea, and it rains A LOT in Providence (regardless of the season). Like literally on average about 3 days a week. So invest in rainboots and a good raincoat and umbrella. Other than that, you'll be fine. I LOVE PROVIDENCE WEATHER!

Q Rain.

There is a lot of rain and not very good drainage so definitely a lot of flooding in the street. If it rains it rains for large chunks of time.

Q Horrible Weather

The weather in providence is always unpredictable, yet it usually gets very cold.

Q SUCKS

Freezing rain and high speed winds really keeps students indoors and makes me not want to go ANYWHERE beyond my dorm. The few weeks of nice weather in September and April/May are definitely not enough to cover for the crappy cold rain and wind October to March.

Q The first years treated me well. This past year I got fed up with it. Preparing to come here, my parents bought me snow gloves and snow pants. I think I wore my snow pants once in three years.

Q The weather is the same as New York's, except it's bitter cold and rain boots are must here because the drainage system is horrible in Providence.

Q The winter in Providence is brutal. It is really cold and nothing like California weather at all.

Q Winter can be rough with a lot of wintry mixes. Invest in rubber boots or you'll go through two or three pairs of shoes every winter kicking your way through slush in the streets. That being said, when it's not precipitating, the weather is fairly mild and easy to deal with.

The College Prowler Take On...
Weather

In Providence, it seems to rain two out of three days, or it snows a ton. Some days in Providence are absolutely stunning, and if you visit in May, you'll probably see hundreds of students frolicking on the green. Everyone looks deliriously happy because this is one of the dozen perfect days of the year. Some winters, there are particularly heavy snow falls, which cause the school to close down for a day or two. When it's not snowing, it can be bitterly cold and depressing as the sun sets before 5 p.m. for a few months in the winter.

But most students adjust to the weather. Rain and snow-resistant clothes are a staple of every student's wardrobe. Heating in the dorms is fine, but the old houses that students inhabit off campus don't always have central heating, and gas and electricity bills run high in the cold months. While the weather is nothing to prevent anyone from coming to Brown, it is something that you must be prepared to deal with.

The College Prowler® Grade on
Weather: C

A high Weather grade designates that temperatures are mild and rarely reach extremes, that the campus tends to be sunny rather than rainy, and that weather is fairly consistent rather than unpredictable.

BROWN UNIVERSITY

Report Card Summary

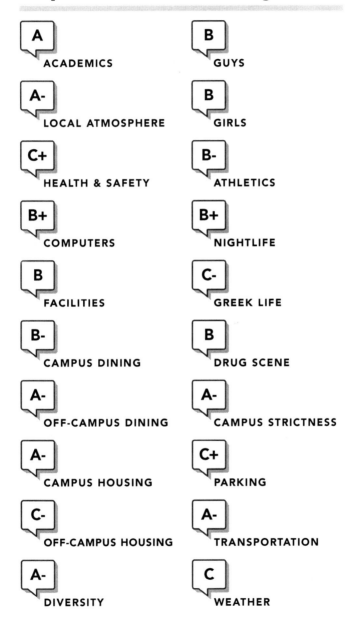

A ACADEMICS	**B** GUYS
A- LOCAL ATMOSPHERE	**B** GIRLS
C+ HEALTH & SAFETY	**B-** ATHLETICS
B+ COMPUTERS	**B+** NIGHTLIFE
B FACILITIES	**C-** GREEK LIFE
B- CAMPUS DINING	**B** DRUG SCENE
A- OFF-CAMPUS DINING	**A-** CAMPUS STRICTNESS
A- CAMPUS HOUSING	**C+** PARKING
C- OFF-CAMPUS HOUSING	**A-** TRANSPORTATION
A- DIVERSITY	**C** WEATHER

Overall Experience

Students Speak Out On...
Overall Experience

Q **Brown - The Best IVY**
I decided that I will go to Brown, after my sixth grade.
Something fascinated me about Browm. Before email
was everywhere, my dad, always the techie type, was
connected to the net. Anyway, I wrote to Brown about what
it will take to get there. They replied with a canned answer.
needles to sya that I got in and was wait-listed at Harvard.
After one semester at Brown, I couldn't have chosen a
perfect school for myself. Brown is nuturing and a great
school and to me, it is the best of the IVYs.

ℚ Brown Is the Best!

Brown is not a huge party school, nor is it a drive-you-into-the-ground academic school. It's a place designed for people who care about intellect and social justice.

ℚ What Makes My School Unique

Brown has the open curriculum, which gives many students the opportunity to try out new things. As a freshman, I took a musical theatre class pass/fail, which was something new to me. It was a great class, and I learned many interesting things about musical theatre. The diversity on campus is also really unique. Compared to other campuses, I think Brown has a very different mix of students from different backgrounds.

ℚ I Love School

Brown is the best college ever. Obviously you need to balance your academics with extracurricular activities and your social life. At the end of the day, it is highly important to remember that the reason to be at college is to get a degree. My favorite experience probably was freshman orientation. There was so much going on, and everyone was so helpful and friendly. My school is unique because it allows your to be yourself, and doesn't penalize you for legal displays of your personal character. If I had the choice all over again, I would choose Brown for every time asked.

ℚ

I indulged my social life and my academic life. It was amazingly liberating. I think I'm leaving Brown knowing who I am and where I want to go. I don't have the specific plan, but I have the ability to deal with it. I think that's pretty specific to Brown. Everyone here has a good sense of themselves. They go through their life at Brown and are comfortable with themselves after.

ℚ

Brown is an Ivy League school that places more emphasis on the quality of a liberal education than on the way they are perceived by other schools. Therefore, students at Brown are generally not competitive with each other; they do not feel the need to define their credibility by their GPA. Instead, Brown students are known for choosing to study what truly interests them, uninfluenced by economic or social pressures.

Q The freedom of Brown's curriculum encourages a versatile education and allows students to have complete discretion when it comes to course and concentration selection.

Q Given the choice to do it over again, I would definitely come to Brown. Before I came to college, I never thought that the size of the school would be something really important to me. Now I know I would never want to go to a school that was any bigger. I think the size really lets you get to know a lot of people here. All my friends who just graduated are depressed that they're leaving. I have friends at other schools who are thrilled to be getting out after four years.

The College Prowler Take On...
Overall Experience

Brown has a reputation that precedes itself. As an Ivy League school, Brown carries a distinction that many students desire, while knowing little about what they need or want in a liberal arts education. In that sense, Brown's liberal nature and open curriculum exceed that of the average liberal arts school. Many students redefine and rediscover themselves in college, and Brown's biggest strength is that it promotes individual development and self-discovery over the course of the undergraduate career. Internally, you have a lot of chances to make mistakes, which the University calls "discoveries," in the course of your studies. It's easy to change your concentration in the fifth or even sixth semester.

Few people who choose Brown regret it. While it's not the school for everyone, almost anyone can find what they are looking for at Brown. Whether you are from New England or Siberia, there are clubs, organizations, classes, and fellow students who share your academic and personal interests. Most people choose Brown for its liberal nature and its strong academic resources, and few are disappointed.

The Inside Scoop

The Lowdown On...
The Inside Scoop

School Slang

BDH: The Brown Daily Herald, Brown's daily paper.

BUPD: Brown University Police Department, including everything from police reports to parking issues.

CAP: Curricular Advising Program, all first-years enter a CAP course as a way to gain exposure to academic advising at the University.

CIS: Computer and Information Services, provides e-mail, voicemail, and more.

CIT: Center for Information Technology, a landmark for directions at the center of campus and one of Brown's main computer clusters.

The Corporation: The Brown Corporation, which owns the school and runs many of its higher level functions

DOC: A dean of the college.

EMS: Emergency Medical Services, provides support for any medical emergency.

The Gate: Pembroke on-campus restaurant that accepts meal credit.

GISP: Group Independent Study Project, student-created group class.

ISP: Independent Study Project, student-created independent class.

Jo's: Nickname for Josiah's restaurant on campus.

Josiah Carberry: Mythical professor of psychoceramics.

LASO: Latin American Student Organization.

Meiklejohns: First-year peer academic councelors.

MPC: Minority Peer Councilors, one of three support counselors in first-year dorms.

OMAC: The main sports facility on campus.

OUAP: Organization of United African Peoples, umbrella organization that addresses concerns of students.

PLME: Program in Liberal Medical Education.

R/ASC: Resource/Academic Support Center.

Randall Counselors: Academic advisors for sophomores.

Ratty: The Sharpe Refractory, the main dining hall.

RC: Residential Councelor, one of three counselors in freshmen dorms.

The Rock: Rockefeller Library

RP: Residence Programmers, upperclassmen dorm programmers.

SAAB: Student Athletic Advisory Board.

SciLi: The Sciences Library.

SDS: Students for a Democratic Society

TNT: The Next Thing, a support group for the LGBTA.

TWC & TWTP: Third World Center and Third World Transition Program.

UDC: University Disciplinary Council.

UFS: University Food Services, handles meal plan issues.

UTRA: Undergraduate Teaching and Research Assistantships, a research grant offered to students.

V-Dub: The Verney-Woolley dining hall.

WiSE: Women in Science and Engineering program.

WPC: Women Peer Counselors, one of three councelors in freshmen dorms.

Things I Wish I Knew Before Coming To School

• Be careful of the credit/no credit grade option. Usually, you end up getting an A anyway, or you totally slack off and get nothing out of the class.

• If you are coming from a warm area, don't underestimate the cold of the winter here. Be sure to buy a thick, warm, water-resistant winter coat.

• Most things can be bought at school for about the same cost as shipping, so don't be a pack rat when you are moving to campus.

• Upper-level courses are not necessarily harder than lower level ones. Don't be afraid to take harder classes as a freshman if you are interested in them.

• What you take freshman year doesn't matter, but your grades do.

Tips to Succeed

• Always seek the council of an advisor or a dean if you need questions answered or if you are having a hard time. Deans, especially, are there to protect you when things go wrong and can help improve your overall Brown experience.

• Be persistent, whether dealing with classes or any other University service.

• Don't overload yourself. Take some time the first semester or two to work your way into the lifestyle and see what you can handle. Even if the classes are not particularly difficult, it is very easy to get overwhelmed by all of the new things going on when you first start.

• Make connections with professors or administrators who can provide good recommendations for you.

Traditions

The "Inverted Sock" Graduation Loop: Famed among University graduation processionals, the "Inverted Sock" walk down College Hill for commencement is a brilliant scheme that allows alumni, professors, and the graduating class to pass each other twice in the mile-long walk to the First Baptist Church of Providence, where the graduation ceremony occurs.

ADOCH (A Day on College Hill): All admitted students are invited to participate in ADOCH, a two-day event in April where pre-frosh from all over the world come to check out the University and meet for the first time. While it's not required, it's the first chance for many students to meet their fellow classmates for the coming year. It's also when a lot of potential students decide to come to Brown.

Campus Dance : During graduation, the campus dance is a centerpiece event where graduating seniors, alumni, families, professors, and underclassmen all come together to waltz and drink on the paper-lantern lit Main Green in front of a live band.

The Freshman Ice Cream Social: The ice cream social on the terrace of Andrews Dorm during the first week of freshman year is a great chance for people to come out of their dorm rooms and meet other first-years.

The Gala: The spring Gala is a campus-wide event where students don their fancy rented tuxedos and escort their date to an evening of dancing in a ballroom downtown. Students rent limos or buses, dine in Providence's fanciest restaurants, and dance and party at one of Brown's biggest campus-wide student events. If you missed prom in high school, it's a great second chance.

Senior Week: The week before graduation is the last chance for seniors to celebrate before leaving the University. Underclassmen are invited to stick around in certain dorms while they work or party at the events. The week includes the campus dance, commencement ceremonies, special nights at clubs and bars, and some of the wildest parties of the year.

Spring Weekend: Usually timed to coincide with the burst of green that happens in late April, spring weekend promises a few solid rock or hip-hop shows, frat boys on couches at the greens, and people wearing smiles, shorts, and bikinis. It's a chance to cut loose before final exams.

The Van Winkle Gate: Every student walks through the main gates of the University exactly twice in their undergraduate career. The first week of freshman year, the gates are swung inwards toward University Hall, inviting new University members to enter the Brown campus. Years later, upon graduating, the gates are opened out, ushering the grads back into the world and ceremoniously ending their time at Brown.

Urban Legends

• If a student walks through the Van Wickle gates after entering the school but before graduating, he/she will not graduate.

• If guys step on the Pembroke seal, they will never graduate. If girls step on it, they will become pregnant.

• Josiah Carberry is the fabled professor of psychoceramics (cracked pots) at the University. Many things around campus, such as Josiah's café and the Brown online library catalog are named after him.

• There are several secret societies at Brown.

• There is a book bound in human leather in the John Hay Special Collections Library.

Students Speak Out On...
The Inside Scoop

Q Student Independence and Rigor

Since Brown has an open curriculum, students have to have the independence and motivation to structure their own course of study. This is what sets Brown apart for all other colleges! The open curriculum is one of the main reasons students choose to come to Brown. At the same time, a Brown education is rigorous no matter what path a student chooses. I think that is the mark of an astounding institution - student choice AND rigor!

Q Two Words: Open Curricular!

I absolutely love the open curricular. I am free to take any class I would like!

Q The Pitfalls. Brown Is NOT One-Size-Fits-All.

You'll do everything for your resume, even if you're SURE you're not that kind of kid. Trust me, you become that kid. Just be prepared for that. Meanwhile, we're meant to be "laid back," so we have to pretend not to be competitive. Everyone seems to think classes come second to extracurriculars. And everyone is trying to everything to live up to the Brown "interesting people" reputation, with the result that no one can commit to anything because we're all doing everything. At the end of the day, we don't know how to talk to each other about the things we care about. And Providence is SO dull.

Jobs & Internships

The Lowdown On...
Jobs & Internships

Employment Services?
Yes

Placement Services?
Yes

Other Career Services
Career counseling interviews
with Brown alumni
Job-hunting workshops
Mock Interviews
Résumé building
Standardized test preparation

Advice

There are a few good ways to get good work around the University. An easy and surefire option is to work for the University Food and Catering Service or the library system, both of which hire students for all shifts and give good hours with decent pay. For a more academic job, most professors hire students as research or administrative assistants, depending on the department. Students can get these by taking classes with the professor and demonstrating genuine interest and ability in the course, as well as developing a relationship with the professor.   Brown has the typical support to aid students looking for jobs and internships. The place to start is the Career Services Center, which offers a full range of resources to students. They have a library with walls of books for researching internships, grants, programs, and job opportunities. The staff reviews and edits résumés and cover letters and they perform mock interviews. Others include the dossier service, which keeps recommendations on file for students and a Web site that lists jobs and internships. In the end, however, most students use Career Services sparingly and have limited results actually finding jobs through the network. Going to career services, however, can be a great way to get motivated or receive specific advice about cover letters or résumés.

Firms That Most Frequently Hire Grads

Bain and Co.
Corporate Executive Board
Goldman Sachs
Google
Harvard University
Microsoft
Morgan Stanley
Peace Corps
Rhode Island Hospital
Teach for America

Alumni & Post-Grads

The Lowdown On...
Alumni & Post-Grads

Alumni Office
Maddock Alumni Center
Across from Wayland Arch
Phone: (401) 863-7070
alumni_relations@brown.edu
www.alumni.brown.edu

Major Alumni Events
Commencement

Services Available
Alumni College Advising
Alumni Directory

Alumni Medical and Home
Insurance
Career Networking

Alumni Publications
B2B: Brown News for Brown
Alumni, sent monthly by
e-mail offering alumni
connections, campus news
headlines, sports news, and
other on-campus events
BAM, Brown Alumni
Magazine, published six

times annual and mailed
to all alumni with active
addresses

Did You Know?

Famous Brown Alumni:
John D. Rockefeller, Jr. (Class of 1897) –
Philanthropist, son of John D. Rockefeller
Charles Evans Hughes (Class of 1910) – Former
Supreme Court justice

Robert Conley (Class of 1953) – Founder of NPR

Ted Turner (Class of 1960) – Media mogul

John F. Kennedy, Jr. (Class of 1983) – Son of John F. Kennedy

Todd Haynes (Class of 1985) – Writer/director

Laura Linney (Class of 1986) – Academy Award nominated actress

Lisa Loeb (Class of 1990) – Singer/songwriter

Duncan Sheik (Class of 1992) – Singer/songwriter

Student Organizations

The Lowdown On...

ROTC
Air Force ROTC: No
Navy ROTC: No
Army ROTC: No

Student Activities Offered

African Students Association (ASA)

African Sun

American Civil Liberties Union (ACLU)

American Medical Student Association Pre-Med chapter (AMSA)

Amnesty International

Animal Rights Coalition, Brown (BARC)

Anime Brunonia

Arab-American Anti-Discrimination Committee (AADC)

ARRR!!!

Art Forum

Asian American Student Association (AASA)

Ballroom Dance Club, Brown (BBDC)

Ballroom Dance Team (BBDT)

Band, Brown (Brown Band)

Bear Necessities, The (TBN)

Beasts of Funny

Best Buddies at Brown

Big Brothers at Brown

Bio-medical Engineering Society (BMES)

Bowling Club (College Hill)

Break Dancing Club

Brotherhood, The

Brown'sTones

Bruin Club

Bruinettes Dance Team, The Brown

Campus Alliance to End Gun Violence (CAEGV)

Cape Verdean Student Association

Catalyst, The

Catholic Pastoral Council at Brown

Celtic Cultural Organization

Chattertocks (TOCKS)

Chess Club at Brown

Chinese Students Association (CSA)

Christian Fellowship, Brown (BCF)

Clerestory

Coalition for Social Justice (CSJ)

Coalition of Bands at Brown (COBAB)

College Democrats at Brown

College Hill for Christ (CHC)

College Hill Independent (Indy)

College Republicans at Brown

Common Ground

Computer Network Management Group (CONMAG)

Concert Agency, Brown (BCA)

Concilio Latino, El

Contra and Folk Dance Society

Cooking & Baking Club

Cricket Club at Brown

Critical Review

Cultural Activities Board (CAB)

Cycling Club at Brown

Dead White Men: A Festival of Classics

Debate
Derbies, Brown
Economic Review, Brown
Enchor Singers, Brown
Engineering Society
Entrepreneurship Program
Environmental Action
Network
Fantasy Gaming Society
(FGS)
FBI, The
Federacion de Estudiantes
Puertorriquenos, La (FEP)
Feminist Majority Leadership
Alliance (FMLA)
Field Hockey Club
Filipino Alliance (FA)
Film Society, Brown (BFS)
Flying Club
Free the Children
Friends of Turkey
Fuerza Latina, La
Fusion Dance Company
Go Association, Brown
Gospel Voices of Praise
Greek Council
Green Party
Habitat for Humanity, Brown
University Chapter
Harmonic Motion
Hawaii Club
Hellenic Students Association
(HSA)
Higher Keys
Hi-T
Hong Kong Students
Association (HKSA)
Hourglass Cafe
IMPROVidence
Independent Artist Network

International Organisation,
Brown (BRIO)
International Socialist
Organization (ISO)
Investment Group, Brown
Issues
Jabberwocks (WOCKS)
Japanese Cultural
Association (JCA)
Jewish Student Union (JSU)
Journal of World Affairs,
Brown (BJWA)
Jug, The Brown
Juggling Club, Out of Hand
(OOH)
Kempo Club, Brown
Key Club, Brown
Kick Boxing Club
Korean Adoptee Mentoring
Program
Korean American Students
Association (KASA)
Latin American Students
Organization (LASO)
Lecture Board, Brown
Lesbian, Gay, Bisexual, and
Transgendered Alliance
(LGBTA)
Linux Users Group, Brown
(BLUG)
Lion Dance, Brown
Madrigal Singers, Brown
Mandarin Enrichment,
Student Association
Mediation Project, Brown
University (BUMP)
Men's Club Soccer
Men's Club Tennis
Men's Lacrosse
Men's Ultimate Team at

Brown
Merlions
MEZCLA
Mock Trial Club
Model United Nations Club
Movimiento Estudantil
Chicano de Aztlan, El
(MEChA)
Musical Forum
Muslim Students Association,
Brown (BMSA)
National Society of Black
Engineers (NSBE)
Native Americans at Brown
(NAB)
Next Thing, The (TNT)
Not Another Victim
Anywhere (NAVA)
Nuestra Gente Mexicana
Online Gaming Society at
Brown
ONYX
Organization of Multiracial
and Biracial Students, Brown
(BOMBS)
Organization of United
African Peoples (OUAP)
Organization of Women
Leaders (OWL)
Original Music Group
Orthodox Christian
Fellowship
Out of Bounds
Outing Club at Brown
Oxfam at Brown
Pakistani Society at Brown
(PSAB)
Photo Club at Brown
Production Workshop (PW)
Program in Liberal Medical

Education Senate
Undergraduate (PLME)
Reformed University
Fellowship
Resumed Undergraduate
Students Association (RUSA)
Shades of Brown
Shakespeare on the Green
Shotokan Karate Club, Brown
University (BUSKC)
Sisters United, Brown
Snowboarding Club at
Brown, the
Society for Clinical Research
for Undergraduates at Brown
(SCRUB)
Somos (Latino Literary
Magazine)
Soul Cypher
South Asian Students
Association (SASA)
Space Club at Brown
Special Events Committee
(SPEC)
Spectator, Brown
Stand Up Comics, Brown
Student Labor Alliance
Student Radio, Brown (WBSR)
Students Against Acronyms
Students for a Free Tibet
Students for a Sensible Drug
Policy
Students for AIDS Awareness
Students for Choice
Students for Liberty
Students for Life, Brown/RISD
Students for Responsible
Investing
Students in Free Enterprise
Students of Caribbean

Ancestry (SOCA)
Students on Financial Aid
(SOFA)
SugarCane
Surf Club, Brown
Swing Club at Brown
Tae Kwon Do Club at Brown
Taiwan Society, Brown (BTS)
Tang Soo Do Club
Tap Club
Television, Brown (BTV)
Thai Student Association
(TSA)
Tikkun Itzlach Club
Undergraduate Council of
Students (UCS)
Undergraduate Council of
Students Election Board
Undergraduate Finance
Board (UFB)
Underground, the (UG)
UNICEF Club
Unitarian Universalist
Undergrad Group
Ursa Minors
Vietnamese Student's
Association (VSA)
Winebox Theatre
With One Voice
Women Students at Brown
(WSaB)
Women's Club Soccer
Women's Rugby
Women's Tennis Club
Women's Ultimate
Word Performance Poetry
Group
Yacht Club
Yarmulkazi! (Brown's Klezmer
Band)

Young Americans for
Freedom
Young Communist League
(YCL)
Young Minority Investors
Club
Ze French Club
Zen Community at Brown

The Best

The **BEST** Things

1. The New Curriculum

2. The student body

3. President Ruth Simmons

4. Thayer Street

5. The College Greens

6. The restaurants off campus

7. Cheap rent

8. Close to Boston and New York City

9. Providence

10. The classes and professors

The Worst

The **WORST** Things

1. On-campus cable

2. The paltry endowment

3. Long winters

4. The meal plan

5. Providence parking laws

6. Bars close too early (2 a.m.)

7. No grocery stores within walking distance

8. Fake IDs hardly ever work

9. The stress of the housing lottery

10. Lots of rain

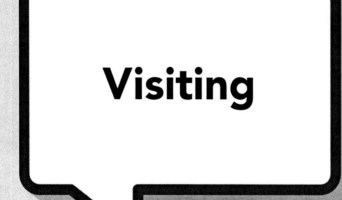

Visiting

The Lowdown On...
Visiting

Campus Tours

Tours are offered most days at varying times in the morning and the evening, and take about an hour. The office recommends contacting them for specific schedules.

Virtual Tour of Campus

www.brown.edu/Students/Bruin_Club/tour/corliss.html

Interviews & Information Sessions

Call (401) 863-2378 on any weekday from 8:30 a.m.–5 p.m. eastern time for information about tours. Interviews are recommended but not required. Off-campus interviews are offered by alumni who contact students applying for admission and arrange a time and place to meet. These interviews provide the Board of Admission with another means with which to evaluate the applicant.

Overnight Visits

A limited number of high school students can stay with current freshmen on weeknights during the semester. This is an excellent way to see first-hand the typical day of a Brown student on campus and in class. Registration is done online at the Admissions Web site.

Words to Know

Academic Probation – A suspension imposed on a student if he or she fails to keep up with the school's minimum academic requirements. Those unable to improve their grades after receiving this warning can face dismissal.

Beer Pong/Beirut – A drinking game involving cups of beer arranged in a pyramid shape on each side of a table. The goal is to get a ping pong ball into one of the opponent's cups by throwing the ball or hitting it with a paddle. If the ball lands in a cup, the opponent is required to drink the beer.

Bid – An invitation from a fraternity or sorority to 'pledge' (join) that specific house.

Blue-Light Phone – Brightly-colored phone posts with a blue light bulb on top. These phones exist for security purposes and are located at various outside locations around most campuses. In an emergency, a student can pick up one of these phones (free of charge) to connect with campus police or a security escort.

Campus Police – Police who are specifically assigned to a given institution. Campus police are typically not regular city officers; they are employed by the university in a full-time capacity.

Club Sports – A level of sports that falls somewhere between varsity and intramural. If a student is unable to commit to a varsity team but has a lot of passion for athletics, a club sport could be a better, less intense option. Even less demanding, intramural (IM) sports often involve no traveling and considerably less time.

Cocaine – An illegal drug. Also known as "coke" or "blow," cocaine often resembles a white crystalline or powdery substance. It is highly addictive and dangerous.

Common Application – An application with which students can apply to multiple schools.

Course Registration – The period of official class selection for the upcoming quarter or semester. Prior to registration, it is best to prepare several back-up courses in case a particular class becomes full. If a course is full, students can place themselves on the waitlist, although this still does not guarantee entry.

Division Athletics – Athletic classifications range from Division I to Division III. Division IA is the most competitive, while Division III is considered to be the least competitive.

Dorm – A dorm (or dormitory) is an on-campus housing facility. Dorms can provide a range of options from suite-style rooms to more communal options that include shared bathrooms. Most first-year students live in dorms. Some upperclassmen who wish to stay on campus also choose this option.

Early Action – An application option with which a student can apply to a school and receive an early acceptance response without a binding commitment. This system is becoming less and less available.

Early Decision – An application option that students should use only if they are certain they plan to attend the school in question. If a student applies using the early decision option and is admitted, he or she is required and bound to attend that university. Admission rates are usually higher among students who apply through early decision, as the student is clearly indicating that the school is his or her first choice.

Ecstasy – An illegal drug. Also known as "E" or "X," ecstasy looks like a pill and most resembles an aspirin. Considered a party drug, ecstasy is very dangerous and can be deadly.

Ethernet – An extremely fast Internet connection available in most university-owned residence halls. To use an Ethernet connection properly, a student will need a network card and cable for his or her computer.

Fake ID – A counterfeit identification card that contains false information. Most commonly, students get fake IDs with altered birthdates so that they appear to be older than 21 (and therefore of legal drinking age). Even though it is illegal, many college students have fake IDs in hopes of purchasing alcohol or getting into bars.

Frosh – Slang for "freshman" or "freshmen."

Hazing – Initiation rituals administered by some fraternities or sororities as part of the pledging process. Many universities have outlawed hazing due to its degrading, and sometimes dangerous, nature.

Intramurals (IMs) – A popular, and usually free, sport league in which students create teams and compete against one another. These sports vary in competitiveness and can include a range of activities—everything from billiards to water polo. IM sports are a great way to meet people with similar interests.

Keg – Officially called a half-barrel, a keg contains roughly 200 12-ounce servings of beer.

LSD – An illegal drug, also known as acid, this hallucinogenic drug most commonly resembles a tab of paper.

Marijuana – An illegal drug, also known as weed or pot; along with alcohol, marijuana is one of the most commonly found drugs on campuses across the country.

Major –The focal point of a student's college studies; a specific topic that is studied for a degree. Examples of majors include physics, English, history, computer science, economics, business, and music. Many students decide on a specific major before arriving on campus, while others are simply "undecided" until declaring a major. Those who are extremely interested in two areas can also choose to double major.

Meal Block – The equivalent of one meal. Students on a meal plan usually receive a fixed number of meals per week. Each meal, or "block," can be redeemed at the school's dining facilities in place of cash. Often, a student's weekly allotment of meal blocks will be forfeited if not used.

Minor – An additional focal point in a student's education. Often serving as a complement or addition to a student's main area of focus, a minor has fewer requirements and prerequisites to fulfill than a major. Minors are not required for graduation from most schools; however some students who want to explore many different interests choose to pursue both a major and a minor.

Mushrooms – An illegal drug. Also known as "'shrooms," this drug resembles regular mushrooms but is extremely hallucinogenic.

Off-Campus Housing – Housing from a particular landlord or rental group that is not affiliated with the university. Depending on the college, off-campus housing can range from extremely popular to non-existent. Students who choose to live off campus are typically given more freedom, but they also have to deal with possible subletting scenarios, furniture, bills, and other issues. In addition to these factors, rental prices and distance often affect a student's decision to move off campus.

Office Hours – Time that teachers set aside for students who have questions about coursework. Office hours are a good forum for students to go over any problems and to show interest in the subject material.

Pledging – The early phase of joining a fraternity or sorority, pledging takes place after a student has gone through rush and received a bid. Pledging usually lasts between one and two semesters. Once the pledging period is complete and a particular student has done everything that is required to become a member, that student is considered a brother or sister. If a fraternity or a sorority would decide to "haze" a group of students, this initiation would take place during the pledging period.

Private Institution – A school that does not use tax revenue to subsidize education costs. Private schools typically cost more than public schools and are usually smaller.

Prof – Slang for "professor."

Public Institution – A school that uses tax revenue to subsidize education costs. Public schools are often a good value for in-state residents and tend to be larger than most private colleges.

Quarter System (or Trimester System) – A type of academic calendar system. In this setup, students take classes for three academic periods. The first quarter usually starts in late September or early October and concludes right before Christmas. The second quarter usually starts around early to mid–January and finishes up around March or April. The last academic quarter, or "third quarter," usually starts in late March or early April and finishes up in late May or Mid-June. The fourth quarter is summer. The major difference between the quarter system and semester system is that students take more, less comprehensive courses under the quarter calendar.

RA (Resident Assistant) – A student leader who is assigned to a particular floor in a dormitory in order to help to the other students who live there. An RA's duties include ensuring student safety and providing assistance wherever possible.

Recitation – An extension of a specific course; a review session. Some classes, particularly large lectures, are supplemented with mandatory recitation sessions that provide a relatively personal class setting.

Rolling Admissions – A form of admissions. Most commonly found at public institutions, schools with this type of policy continue to accept students throughout the year until their class sizes are met. For example, some schools begin accepting students as early as December and will continue to do so until April or May.

Room and Board – This figure is typically the combined cost of a university-owned room and a meal plan.

Room Draw/Housing Lottery – A common way to pick on-campus room assignments for the following year. If a student decides to remain in university-owned housing, he or she is assigned a unique number that, along with seniority, is used to determine his or her housing for the next year.

Rush – The period in which students can meet the brothers and sisters of a particular chapter and find out if a given fraternity or sorority is right for them. Rushing a fraternity or a sorority is not a requirement at any school. The goal of rush is to give students who are serious about pledging a feel for what to expect.

Semester System – The most common type of academic calendar system at college campuses. This setup typically includes two semesters in a given school year. The fall semester starts around the end of August or early September and concludes before winter vacation. The spring semester usually starts in mid-January and ends in late April or May.

Student Center/Rec Center/Student Union – A common area on campus that often contains study areas, recreation facilities, and eateries. This building is often a good place to meet up with fellow students; depending on the school, the student center can have a huge role or a non-existent role in campus life.

Student ID – A university-issued photo ID that serves as a student's key to school-related functions. Some schools require students to show these cards in order to get into dorms, libraries, cafeterias, and other facilities. In addition to storing meal plan information, in some cases, a student ID can actually work as a debit card and allow students to purchase things from bookstores or local shops.

Suite – A type of dorm room. Unlike dorms that feature communal bathrooms shared by the entire floor, suites offer bathrooms shared only among the suite. Suite-style dorm rooms can house anywhere from two to ten students.

TA (Teacher's Assistant) – An undergraduate or grad student who helps in some manner with a specific course. In some cases, a TA will teach a class, assist a professor, grade assignments, or conduct office hours.

Undergraduate – A student in the process of studying for his or her bachelor's degree.

About the Author

Name: Justin Kim

Hometown: Austin, TX

Major: Undecided

Fun Fact: Justin ranked internationally in competitive Minesweeper.

Previous Contributors: Matthew Kittay

Pros and Cons

Still can't figure out if this is the right school for you?
You've already read through this in-depth guide;
why not list the pros and cons? It will really help
with narrowing down your decision and determining
whether or not this school is right for you.

Pros	Cons
....	....
....	....
....	....
....	....
....	....
....	....
....	....
....	....
....	....
....	....
....	....

Pros and Cons

Still can't figure out if this is the right school for you?
You've already read through this in-depth guide;
why not list the pros and cons? It will really help
with narrowing down your decision and determining
whether or not this school is right for you.

Pros	Cons
....	....
....	....
....	....
....	....
....	....
....	....
....	....
....	....
....	....
....	....
....	....
....	....

Notes

....

....

....

....

....

....

....

....

....

....

....

....

....

....

....

Notes

....

....

....

....

....

....

....

....

....

....

....

....

....

....

....

Notes

....

....

....

....

....

....

....

....

....

....

....

....

....

....

Notes

....

....

....

....

....

....

....

....

....

....

....

....

....

....

....

Notes

....

....

....

....

....

....

....

....

....

....

....

....

....

....

....

Notes

Notes

....

....

....

....

....

....

....

....

....

....

....

....

....

....

....

....

Notes

....

....

....

....

....

....

....

....

....

....

....

....

....

....

....

Notes

Notes

....

....

....

....

....

....

....

....

....

....

....

....

....

....

....

Notes

....

....

....

....

....

....

....

....

....

....

....

....

....

....

....

Notes

Notes

....

....

....

....

....

....

....

....

....

....

....

....

....

....

....

....

College Scholarships

Search. Apply. Win!

Review Your School!

Let your voice be heard.

Every year, thousands of students take our online survey to share their opinions about campus life.

Now's your chance to help millions of high school students choose the right college for them.

Tell us what life is really like at your school by taking our online survey or even uploading your own photos and videos!

And as our thanks to you for participating in our survey, we'll enter you into a random drawing for our $1,000 Monthly Survey Scholarship!

For more information, check out
www.collegeprowler.com/survey

WWW.COLLEGEPROWLER.COM

Write For Us!

Express your opinion. Get published!

 Interested in being a published author? College Prowler is always on the lookout for current college students across the country to write the guides for their schools.

The contributing author position is a unique opportunity for eager college students to bolster their résumés and portfolios, become published authors both online and in print, and gain tremendous exposure to millions of high school students nationwide.

For more details, visit
www.collegeprowler.com/careers

Albion College
Alfred University
Allegheny College
Alverno College
American Intercontinental
  University Online
American University
Amherst College
Arizona State University
Ashford University
The Art Institute of
  California – Orange
  County
Auburn University
Austin College
Babson College
Ball State University
Bard College
Barnard College
Barry University
Baruch College
Bates College
Bay Path College
Baylor University
Beloit College
Bentley University
Berea College
Binghamton University
Birmingham Southern
  College
Bob Jones University
Boston College
Boston University
Bowdoin College
Bradley University
Brandeis University
Brigham Young University
Brigham Young
  University – Idaho
Brown University
Bryant University
Bryn Mawr College
Bucknell University
Cal Poly Pomona
California College
  of the Arts
California Institute
  of Technology
California Polytechnic
  State University
California State University
  – Monterey Bay
California State University
  – Northridge
California State University
  – San Marcos
Carleton College
Carnegie Mellon University
Case Western Reserve
  University
Catawba College
Catholic University
  of America

Centenary College
  of Louisiana
Centre College
Chapman University
Chatham University
City College of New York
City College of
  San Francisco
Claflin University
Claremont McKenna
  College
Clark Atlanta University
Clark University
Clemson University
Cleveland State University
Colby College
Colgate University
College of Charleston
College of Mount
  Saint Vincent
College of Notre
  Dame of Maryland
College of the Holy Cross
College of William & Mary
College of Wooster
Colorado College
Columbia College Chicago
Columbia University
Concordia University
  – Wisconsin
Connecticut College
Contra Costa College
Cornell College
Cornell University
Creighton University
CUNY Lehman College
CUNY Queens College
CUNY Queensborough
  Community College
Dalton State College
Dartmouth College
Davidson College
De Anza College
Del Mar College
Denison University
DePaul University
DePauw University
Diablo Valley College
Dickinson College
Dordt College
Drexel University
Duke University
Duquesne University
Earlham College
East Carolina University
Eckerd College
El Paso Community
  College
Elon University
Emerson College
Emory University
Fashion Institute of Design
  & Merchandising

Fashion Institute of
  Technology
Ferris State University
Florida Atlantic University
Florida Southern College
Florida State University
Fordham University
Franklin & Marshall
  College
Franklin Pierce University
Frederick Community
  College
Freed-Hardeman
  University
Furman University
Gannon University
Geneva College
George Mason University
George Washington
  University
Georgetown University
Georgia Institute of
  Technology
Georgia Perimeter College
Georgia State University
Germanna Community
  College
Gettysburg College
Gonzaga University
Goucher College
Grinnell College
Grove City College
Guilford College
Gustavus Adolphus
  College
Hamilton College
Hampshire College
Hampton University
Hanover College
Harvard University
Harvey Mudd College
Hastings College
Haverford College
Hillsborough Community
  College
Hofstra University
Hollins University
Howard University
Hunter College (CUNY)
Idaho State University
Illinois State University
Illinois Wesleyan University
Indiana Univ.–Purdue Univ.
  Indianapolis (IUPUI)
Indiana University
Iowa State University
Ithaca College
Jackson State University
James Madison University
Johns Hopkins University
Juniata College
Kansas State University
Kaplan University

Kent State University
Kenyon College
La Roche College
Lafayette College
Lawrence University
Lehigh University
Lewis & Clark College
Linfield College
Los Angeles City College
Los Angeles Valley College
Louisiana College
Louisiana State University
Loyola College in
  Maryland
Loyola Marymount
  University
Loyola University Chicago
Luther College
Macalester College
Macomb Community
  College
Manhattan College
Manhattanville College
Marlboro College
Marquette University
Maryville University
Massachusetts College
  of Art & Design
Massachusetts Institute
  of Technology
McGill University
Merced College
Mercyhurst College
Messiah College
Miami University
Michigan State University
Middle Tennessee
  State University
Middlebury College
Millsaps College
Minnesota State
  University – Moorhead
Missouri State University
Montana State University
Montclair State University
Moorpark College
Mount Holyoke College
Muhlenberg College
New College of Florida
New York University
North Carolina A&T
  State University
North Carolina State
  University
Northeastern University
Northern Arizona
  University
Northern Illinois University
Northwest Florida
  State College
Northwestern College
  – Saint Paul
Northwestern University

Oakwood University
Oberlin College
Occidental College
Oglethorpe University
Ohio State University
Ohio University
Ohio Wesleyan University
Old Dominion University
Onondaga Community
College
Oral Roberts University
Pace University
Palm Beach State College
Penn State Altoona
Penn State Brandywine
Penn State University
Pepperdine University
Pitzer College
Pomona College
Princeton University
Providence College
Purdue University
Radford University
Ramapo College of
New Jersey
Reed College
Rensselaer Polytechnic
Institute
Rhode Island School
of Design
Rhodes College
Rice University
Rider University
Robert Morris University
Rochester Institute
of Technology
Rocky Mountain College
of Art & Design
Rollins College
Rowan University
Rutgers University
Sacramento State
Saint Francis University
Saint Joseph's University
Saint Leo University
Salem College
Salisbury University
Sam Houston State
University
Samford University
San Diego State University
San Francisco State
University
Santa Clara University
Santa Fe College
Sarah Lawrence College
Scripps College
Seattle University
Seton Hall University
Simmons College
Skidmore College
Slippery Rock University
Smith College

South Texas College
Southern Methodist
University
Southwestern University
Spelman College
St. John's College
– Annapolis
St. John's University
St. Louis University
St. Mary's University
St. Olaf College
Stanford University
State University of New
York – Purchase College
State University of New
York at Fredonia
State University of New
York at Oswego
Stetson University
Stevens-Henager College
Stony Brook University
(SUNY)
Susquehanna University
Swarthmore College
Syracuse University
Taylor University
Temple University
Tennessee State University
Texas A&M University
Texas Christian University
Texas Tech
The Community College
of Baltimore County
Towson University
Trinity College (Conn.)
Trinity University (Texas)
Troy University
Truman State University
Tufts University
Tulane University
Union College
University at Albany
(SUNY)
University at Buffalo
(SUNY)
University of Alabama
University of Arizona
University of Arkansas
University of Arkansas
at Little Rock
University of California
– Berkeley
University of
California – Davis
University of
California – Irvine
University of California
– Los Angeles
University of California
– Merced
University of California
– Riverside
University of California
– San Diego

University of California
– Santa Barbara
University of California
– Santa Cruz
University of Central
Florida
University of Chicago
University of Cincinnati
University of Colorado
University of Connecticut
University of Delaware
University of Denver
University of Florida
University of Georgia
University of Hartford
University of Illinois
University of Illinois
at Chicago
University of Iowa
University of Kansas
University of Kentucky
University of Louisville
University of Maine
University of Maryland
University of Maryland
– Baltimore County
University of
Massachusetts
University of Miami
University of Michigan
University of Minnesota
University of Mississippi
University of Missouri
University of Montana
University of Mount Union
University of Nebraska
University of Nevada
– Las Vegas
University of New
Hampshire
University of North
Carolina
University of North
Carolina – Greensboro
University of Notre Dame
University of Oklahoma
University of Oregon
University of Pennsylvania
University of Phoenix
University of Pittsburgh
University of Puget Sound
University of Rhode Island
University of Richmond
University of Rochester
University of San Diego
University of San Francisco
University of South
Carolina
University of South Dakota
University of South Florida
University of Southern
California
University of St
Thomas – Texas

University of Tampa
University of Tennessee
University of Tennessee
at Chattanooga
University of Texas
University of Utah
University of Vermont
University of Virginia
University of Washington
University of Western
Ontario
University of Wisconsin
University of
Wisconsin – Stout
Urbana University
Ursinus College
Valencia Community
College
Valparaiso University
Vanderbilt University
Vassar College
Villanova University
Virginia Commonwealth
University
Virginia Tech
Virginia Union University
Wagner College
Wake Forest University
Warren Wilson College
Washington &
Jefferson College
Washington & Lee
University
Washington University
in St. Louis
Wellesley College
Wesleyan University
West Los Angeles College
West Point Military
Academy
West Virginia University
Western Illinois University
Western Kentucky
University
Wheaton College (Ill.)
Wheaton College (Mass.)
Whitman College
Wilkes University
Willamette University
Williams College
Xavier University
Yale University
Youngstown State
University

CPSIA information can be obtained at www.ICGtesting.com
Printed in the USA
BVOW021202050612

291830BV00005B/10/P